BUILDING COMMUNITY

NEW APARTMENT ARCHITECTURE

Michael Webb

With 348 illustrations

BUILDING COMMUNITY

NEW APARTMENT ARCHITECTURE

 Thames & Hudson

CONTENTS

Michael Webb is a Los Angeles–based writer who has authored more than twenty books on architecture and design, most recently *Modernist Paradise: Niemeyer House, Boyd Collection* and *Venice, CA: Art + Architecture in a Maverick Community*, while contributing essays to many more. He is also a regular contributor to leading journals in the United States and Europe. Growing up in London, he wrote for *The Times* and *Country Life* before moving to the US to direct film programs for the American Film Institute and curate a Smithsonian exhibition, *Hollywood: Legend and Reality*, which traveled to major American cities and Tokyo.

Front cover: Torr Kaelan, San Diego (see page 134)
Back cover: Sky Habitat, Singapore (see page 232)
Frontispiece: Tietgen Student Hall, Copenhagen (see page 112)

First published in the United Kingdom in 2017 by Thames & Hudson Ltd, 181a High Holborn, London WC1V 7QX

Building Community: New Apartment Architecture
© 2017 Thames & Hudson Ltd, London

Text © 2017 Michael Webb

Illustrations © 2017 the copyright holders; see page 252

Designed by Praline

British Library Cataloguing-in-Publication Data
A catalogue record for this book is available from the British Library

ISBN 978-0-500-34330-2

Printed and bound in China by C & C Offset Printing Co. Ltd

To find out about all our publications, please visit **www.thamesandhudson.com**. There you can subscribe to our e-newsletter, browse or download our current catalogue, and buy any titles that are in print.

Introduction

EVOLUTION OF A TYPOLOGY

When Charles and Ray Eames presented their initial design for one of the Case Study houses (a program of model residences in Southern California sponsored by *Arts & Architecture* magazine in the two postwar decades), they identified themselves as "apartment dwellers." This designing couple proposed a single story of living areas, projecting into space and supported on slender columns. Mies van der Rohe had come up with the same idea, and so, to avoid a charge of plagiarism, Charles amended his design to create the now iconic double-height house with a sleeping gallery over the kitchen and a separate studio. The Eameses relocated from their classic Richard Neutra apartment in the Westwood district of Los Angeles on Christmas Eve 1949, and each wrote a letter to the architect telling him how rewarding it had been to live in his creation.

For nearly forty years, I have had the pleasure of living in that same hilltop apartment. Eight units are grouped around a landscaped courtyard, stepped up the steep slope and accessed from a central staircase. When they were completed in 1937, these white stucco cubes with flat roofs and ribbon windows were a startling apparition in a nascent village of Spanish revival houses. Prospective tenants went away muttering "moon architecture." But a few celebrities, including Orson Welles, Dolores del Río, and the Oscar-winning actress Luise Rainer, moved in, valuing the isolation and privacy of these well-planned apartments, with their abundant natural light and cross-ventilation. Rainer also wrote to Neutra, telling him that she had previously been afraid of modernism, but now enjoyed a great feeling of serenity, gazing out at the views of hills and ocean. Although the apartments were built inexpensively to generate rental income during the Great Depression, they are still highly desirable, even as quiet residential streets have turned into a noisy quarter of student rooming houses.

Like Rainer and the Eameses, I feel perfectly at home here. Trees in the courtyard have matured, providing shade and screening out eyesores. It is easy to imagine oneself in a tree house, and the windows pull in cooling breezes from the ocean. Nothing could be simpler or more satisfying, but far too few architects and developers have followed Neutra's lead. This, despite the fact that, as houses and buildable plots of land become ever less affordable in cities around the world, most people are choosing or being compelled to live in apartments.

There is an urgent need to build many more apartments—to relieve an acute shortage of housing, to use land more economically, to save the energy wasted on long commutes to distant suburbs, and to revitalize cities abandoned by an earlier generation. Indeed, from Sydney to Los Angeles, young people are moving back into urban centers and giving them a fresh jolt of energy. The very notion of suburbia has been discredited as a wasteful delusion: neither city nor countryside, increasingly isolated by traffic congestion.

Multiple housing in urban centers is clearly a better option. But, even as rents and condominium prices soar, the choices remain depressingly narrow. Nearly all apartments are shoehorned into generic blocks and towers: faceless, placeless, and differing only in the expense of the decorative veneer. Claustrophobic cells, as uniform as those in a cheap hotel, open off double-loaded corridors. Light and air come from one side only, and balconies are usually vestigial. "Luxury," a word beloved by property owners, has lost all its meaning: upscale condos are nearly as uniform, cramped, and shoddy as those endured by mere mortals. Kenneth Frampton, a New Yorker by adoption and a leading historian of modernism, admitted, "I have never lived in a modern building of quality in my entire life, never."

In Barcelona, Antoni Gaudí's Casa Milà (1906–10) conceals its steel structure behind undulating waves of stone and wrought-iron balustrades.

Henri Sauvage completed the first of his stepped-back apartment buildings in 1913 in the 6th arrondissement of Paris, using white tile to connote hygiene.

Auguste Perret built the first reinforced-concrete apartment building (1903–04) in the fashionable 16th arrondissement of Paris, cladding the structure in decorative tiles.

Risk-averse developers, concerned only with making a quick profit, seek an easy way through the labyrinth of municipal regulations, and a chorus of Nimbyism greets every departure from the norm. The box, horizontal or vertical, is always a safe option. A few glimmers of creativity relieve the gloom. Social housing, even shelter for the homeless, has challenged idealists to break out of the box, and augment minimal interiors with shared spaces and greenery. From low-rise urban villages to terraced towers, there are scattered initiatives at every level of size and price. Some buildings reach out to the neighborhood, others open up to leafy courtyards. Rigorous geometries alternate with expressive forms that create urban sculptures and shape the living spaces within.

I have selected thirty recent examples from around the world to demonstrate the huge but largely unrealized potential of the apartment building. There is a mix of large and small, tall and ground-hugging, frugal and costly. All were completed in the past ten years, and a few future projects are included in the final chapter. The common thread is creativity: finding new ways to shape and share space while maintaining a balance between community and privacy. These themes are addressed in commentaries by five American and European architects.

Every building, however radical, owes something to its predecessors. As an introduction to the projects that follow, it may be helpful to review a few notable achievements of the 20th century, and explore the evolution of the apartment building as a typology.

Communal living is as old as the first cave dwellings; the single-family house—like the concept of privacy—is a recent invention and one that is likely to become much rarer. In the medieval cities of Europe, everyone lived at close quarters within the straitjacket of the city walls. The upper classes shared their quarters with family and servants; palaces differ from upscale condos in that the most prestigious spaces are on the piano nobile, rather than in the penthouse. Above the state rooms of historic Roman palazzi, distant cousins were ensconced in apartments that feel quite independent of the princely quarters. The poor rarely had a choice. Workers have made do with rickety lodgings from ancient times up to the present day, and the Tenement Museum on New York's Lower East Side reveals how miserably immigrants were housed a century ago. The squalor led to sweeping reforms around 1900 and non-profit housing projects that promoted public health, but even these were often forbidding barracks.

The first middle-class apartments evolved out of townhouses subdivided by families that no longer required or could afford the upper floors, and the first purpose-built apartment buildings resembled mansions in their scale and character. The nine-story block that Auguste Perret completed in 1904 for the use of his family and company offices marked an advance, being the first reinforced-concrete residential building. Located at 25 bis rue Franklin in the newly

Phase two of Eigen Haard (1915–16), a block of workers' apartments designed by Michel de Klerk in the Spaarndammer quarter of Amsterdam.

fashionable 16th arrondissement of Paris, its crisp lines stand out from the heavy masonry blocks to either side. Perret thought it had "the freshness and slenderness of a young girl," but he concealed the concrete behind a floral ceramic skin. The footprint was too small to accommodate the customary interior court, so the center was recessed between projecting side bays. Interior walls are reduced to a minimum, the stairs are pushed to the rear and lit through a wall of glass blocks, and the penthouse that Perret kept for himself opens onto a central terrace. A rationalist in construction (he would direct the rebuilding of war-damaged Le Havre in his final decade), Perret was a traditionalist in his lifelong preference for vertical windows.

Still more deceptive is the Casa Milà of 1906–10 in Barcelona, a masterwork of Antoni Gaudí. Frampton speaks of its "undulating cliff face [and the] perverse suppression of the building's steel structure behind massive stone facing ... to suggest a rock face eroded by time." Concealed within this monument of Catalan Modernisme are spacious apartments with wavy ceilings sculpted by Josep Maria Jujol. It is a habitable work of art that reinterprets the idea of a palace for its multiple occupants, and gives them a rooftop promenade dotted with writhing chimneys, anticipating the fifth façade of Le Corbusier's Unités.

As Gaudí created novel dwellings for the bourgeoisie of Barcelona, reformers in northern European countries were trying to raise the abysmal standards of workers' dwellings. The Dutch Housing Act of 1901 permitted housing associations to be established by churches and trade unions.

Eigen Haard drew fierce criticism from Dutch modernists for its decorative brickwork.

The third, most ambitious block of Eigen Haard was dubbed Het Schip (The Ship, 1917–20) and incorporated a post office, which is now a museum. The spire may have taken its cue from a nearby church.

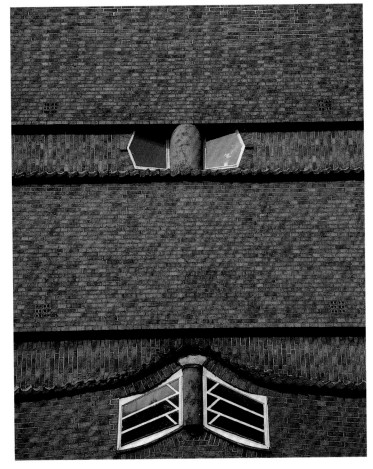

A detail of the Het Schip façade demonstrates de Klerk's love of restrained ornament.

One of these was Eigen Haard (Our Hearth), which commissioned three adjoining blocks (1913–20) in Amsterdam from architect Michel de Klerk. The last of these, Het Schip (The Ship), proved the most controversial in its expressive freedom, richly ornamented brickwork, and bowed spire—a feature that may have been intended as the secular counterpoint to a nearby church. The hundred apartments opened onto the street and a courtyard; a nursery school, meeting hall, and post office (now a small museum) shared the ground floor.

Modernist architects, including Mart Stam and J.J.P. Oud, were fiercely critical of the decorative façades and conventional interiors. City council members complained about the cost but were persuaded that the project would bring them lasting credit. De Klerk went on to design De Dageraad (The Dawn, 1923), which is plainer, save for a corner that rises from the street like a castle keep; and there a municipal subsidy allowed him to design more generous interiors. As he remarked, "Nothing is too good for the worker, who has had to do without beauty for so very long." This sentiment was echoed in a letter from a tenant of Het Schip, which was published in the newspaper *Der Volk* following de Klerk's early death in 1923 at the age of thirty-nine. "It is as if every brick cries out," the writer lamented. "Come all workers and rest from your labors in the homes that await you. Is not the Spaarndammerplein a fairy tale dreamt of as a child, as something we children never had?"

In France, Henri Sauvage pioneered the concept of stepped-back apartment blocks to pull in more light and fresh

The Isokon flats in north London were designed
by Wells Coates in 1933.

The Isokon's original clients, Jack and Molly Pritchard, lived in the penthouse.

The present owner of the penthouse has filled it with the Pritchards' molded plywood furniture.

air and give everyone a private terrace. The first of these was a small infill completed in 1913 on rue Vavin in the 6th arrondissement of Paris. Its concrete frame is clad in glazed and beveled stoneware tiles, the underside of the terraces are gracefully curved, and the shiny expanses of white are highlighted with dark-blue squares in a nod to the buildings of Otto Wagner in Vienna. The taut skin gives the façade a crisp, timeless character, softened by exuberant plantings. Hard to believe it is a century old. This model led on to a much larger project for working-class tenants on rue Amiraux in the 13th arrondissement (1916–26). It is also clad in white tiles—an emblem of hygiene borrowed from tuberculosis sanatoria—and the huge block contains a light well rising from the glass roof of the ground-floor swimming pool.

As the most industrialized country in Europe, Germany had the greatest need of workers' housing, and as many as 140,000 subsidized units were constructed in a few years in the mid-1920s. The *Siedlungen* (housing estates) of Berlin are triumphs of enlightened design and planning, and five of them were named a UNESCO World Heritage site in 2007. One of the most appealing is the Großsiedlung Britz, also known as the Hufeisensiedlung for the horseshoe of apartments that anchors the radiating terraces. Commissioned by the city council on the grounds of an old manor, it comprises 1,960 units for a potential population of 5,000. It was constructed in six phases, 1925–30, to the designs of Bruno Taut and Martin Wagner—an architect who was also an urban development councilor. Modest but well-planned stucco-faced apartments alternate with row houses, all enlivened by Taut's love of exuberant colors; private gardens flow into an expansive park, shaded by mature trees. It is an idyllic composition, and the interweaving of buildings and nature was further explored in two international housing projects in Berlin: the Hansaviertel of 1955–57 and Tegeler Hafen of 1985–88. Both were the product of Cold War rivalry and the desire to make West Berlin a showcase of progressive ideas, in contrast to the regimented developments on the other side of the wall.

Britain pioneered rational town planning and humane housing from the 18th century on, but the penguins of London Zoo were among the first beneficiaries of modern architecture, with their pool designed by Berthold Lubetkin's Tecton Group. Emigré architects—from Europe and the British Empire—led the way in the 1930s, notably with the Lawn Road flats of 1933–34 in the London borough of Camden. Christened "Isokon" for the molded plywood company of the clients, Jack and Molly Pritchard, they were designed

by the Canadian architect Wells Coates. German planners coined the term *Existenzminimum* to describe tiny dwellings with meticulously planned kitchens and bathrooms, and that was the inspiration at Lawn Road.

The four stories of apartments, accessed from outside galleries, seem to be carved from a solid block of concrete, painted a pinkish white. Walter Gropius and Marcel Breuer, en route from Berlin to Harvard, lived here briefly, and Isokon has always appealed to mavericks; it was even home to a nest of Soviet spies in the 1950s. The Pritchards lived in style in the plywood-paneled penthouse that opens onto a private roof terrace, and the designer who now owns the space has furnished it with reissued Isokon furniture. A restaurant-bar was a social hub for residents, and there was a club rule that guests should not have "any religious or other taboos or objectionable opinions that would impede conversation." In 1972, ownership of Isokon passed to Camden Borough Council, which neglected it shamefully; it was given an exemplary restoration by the Notting Hill Housing Association working with Avanti Architects, under the direction of John

The Hufeisensiedlung (1925–30), a workers' housing estate on the western edge of Berlin, takes its name from its horseshoe of apartments at the center of radiating terraces.

Allan, a maestro of modernist conservation. Work was completed in 2004. More recently, the Isokon Gallery, exhibiting the history of this unique building and its distinguished residents, has been created by Allan and his colleagues within the former garage.

The devastation of the Second World War (allied to the backlog of home construction through the Great Depression) galvanized governments and architects throughout Europe. The two postwar decades were an era of idealism, tempered by austerity and a sclerotic bureaucracy that stifled innovation while allowing a body of achievement that today seems

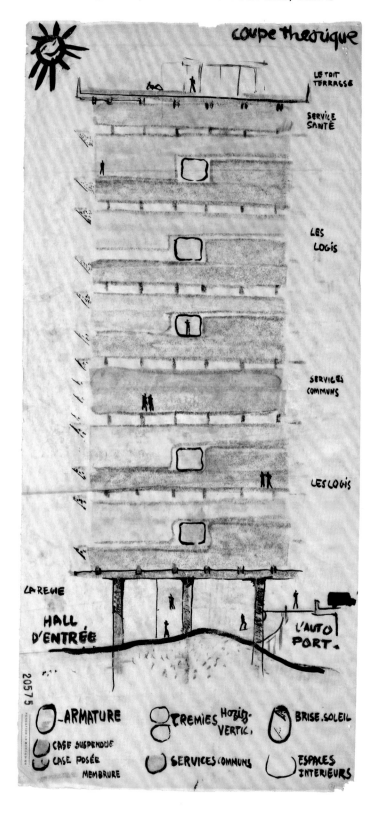

Le Corbusier's lateral section of the first Unité d'Habitation (opposite) shows the split-level configuration of the apartments.

almost miraculous. As early as 1924, Le Corbusier had proposed a Ville Radieuse of tower blocks set in parkland, to replace what he saw as dark and oppressive row housing. That model had a huge impact, for good and ill, on postwar developments in Europe and the Americas.

It took Corbusier until 1947 to secure approval of his first Unité d'Habitation in Marseille, a single twelve-story block that was not completed until 1952. His elevated rhetoric should have swayed the skeptics: "to provide with silence and solitude before the sun, space and greenery a dwelling that will be the perfect receptacle for the family ... and a magisterial work of architecture; the product of rigor, grandeur, nobility, happiness and elegance." In fact, his limited success depended on the support of one champion, Raul Dautry, minister of reconstruction and urbanism, who sponsored an experimental government-funded project to house state employees. As historian Tim Benton recounts, Corbu was allowed to bypass housing regulations and exceed standard budgets—favors that infuriated jealous peers. Reactionaries, who were even more numerous then than now, christened it "La Maison du Fada" ("House of the Loony") even before ground was broken.

All turned out well in Marseille. Rough board-marked concrete, employed to disguise the shortcomings of construction, gave the Unité its heroic character, and the roofscape is a captivating sculpture garden, as well as a prized amenity for residents. There are 337 apartments in twenty-five different configurations, for couples up to families with five children. The split-level section gives most apartments a view of the Mediterranean and the mountains, while allowing for cross-ventilation and shifts in room height. It also reduces the number of internal corridors to one for every three levels. Corbu envisaged a self-sufficient community of 1,600 with a mid-level shopping street, but the demand proved inadequate to support retail outlets. That floor now accommodates visiting aficionados in a frugal but well-run hotel and an exemplary restaurant. Vans bring meat and groceries to residents at the main entrance. The park has become a parking lot, with motorcycles thronging the undercroft, but the residents (who now own their apartments) seem happy, and the Unité has become—along with its four scattered siblings—the most famous and influential apartment block in the world.

In Britain, many postwar council estates took their cues from Corbusier's later work. Berthold Lubetkin, a Georgian who left Moscow in the early 1920s for Berlin and Paris, arrived in London in 1931 and established the firm of Tecton with Francis Skinner, Denys Lasdun, and others. From the Penguin Pool, they graduated to an innovative health center and the Highpoint apartment towers in the Highgate area of London, which prepared these progressive architects for the challenges of postwar housing. It was an unprecedented opportunity to enrich lives, but hedged by budgetary and regulatory constraints. "Architecture should not be judged just by a single house or a block of flats, but by the whole ensemble," Lubetkin declared. "It is the interrelationship of all the buildings together that reveals the aims of the community, expresses the social framework, and gives it its life."

As John Allan recounts in his definitive biography of Lubetkin, the architect was determined to realize his vision, despite all the cuts and compromises that were forced upon him. In the six estates he designed in some poorer neighborhoods of London from the early 1940s through the 1950s, he tried to humanize repetitive blocks by using checkerboard patterns of light and dark materials, flush and recessed surfaces. Most of the educational and social facilities that would have fostered a sense of community on these estates were axed, but he was able to indulge his invention in several extraordinary staircases, which, in terms of complexity, rival those of the 17th-century Roman Baroque architect Borromini. There are few better examples of spending money where it shows, and one wonders how many social encounters—even perhaps affairs—have been sparked on these vertiginous circulation routes.

The Lubetkin estates are quite modest in scale, evolving from models that were first proposed before the war. Park Hill in Sheffield, South Yorkshire, is much more ambitious: a British version of the Ville Radieuse. When it was completed in 1960, on a hilly site overlooking the city center, Sheffield was still a smoky hub of the steel industry. Park Hill was designed by two newly graduated architects, Jack Lynn and Ivor Smith, under the direction of J. Lewis Womersley, the dynamic head of the City Architect's Office. A serpentine complex of slab blocks, seven to thirteen stories high, contained a thousand apartments. Like the megastructures that rose all over Britain, from Cumbernauld in Scotland to Robin Hood Gardens in London, it was a bold effort to rehouse working-class families displaced by bomb damage and slum clearance programs.

Park Hill is a showcase of brutalism, with its muscular concrete frame and two levels of exterior decks, 10 ft (3 m) wide, which link the blocks and provide access to duplex apartments. Human movement was taken as the generating principle of the scheme, and the decks are the visible expression of this. They emphasize continuity, and the lower deck runs out at ground level near the top of the slope. Infill panels in two colors enlivened the façades, generous plantings softened the austere grid, and there was a lively mix of amenities, including three pubs, a nursery, a primary school, a chapel, and five children's playgrounds.

Initially popular with tenants, Park Hill fell victim to inadequate maintenance, and was pilloried in the reaction against modernism from the 1970s on. All over Britain and still more in the United States, large publicly sponsored projects were condemned as inhumane and as breeding grounds for crime. In Sheffield, a neighboring estate, Hyde Park, was disfigured; the Kelvin, a second sibling, was demolished. Park Hill was saved by its English Heritage listing—becoming one of the largest protected buildings in Europe. Urban Splash, the Manchester-based developer that has undertaken other design-propelled conversions, took on the challenge of rehabilitation and hired Hawkins/Brown as architects. Blocks were stripped to the frame, which was patched. Precast concrete balustrades were replaced, windows enlarged, and brick infill exchanged for brightly colored anodized aluminum panels. The interiors were upgraded, but a third of the apartments are still reserved for low-income tenants.

The Cité du Lignon, constructed between 1963 and 1971 on farmland outside Geneva, was an even more ambitious response to the postwar housing crisis. Designed by a team of architects led by Georges Addor, it contains 2,780 apartments currently occupied by about 6,800 people,

Le Corbusier completed his first Unité d'Habitation in Marseille in 1952. The apartments are accessed from central corridors on every third floor.

Bevin Court is one of several low-income London housing estates designed by Berthold Lubetkin of Tecton in the decade following the Second World War.

Theatrical staircases, such as this one on the Dorset Estate in Bethnal Green, added distinction to Lubetkin's frugal London projects.

Another of Lubetkin's dramatic staircases, this one on the Cranbrook Estate, also in Bethnal Green.

Oscar Niemeyer designed this sensuously curved apartment tower, Edifício Niemeyer (1954–60, named for his brother), in the Brazilian city of Belo Horizonte.

although it was built to house 10,000. A linear block, twelve to fourteen stories tall and 3,500 ft (1,065 m) long, snakes through the landscape; a pair of tower blocks, twenty-six and thirty stories high, provides vertical emphasis. *Time* magazine described it as "a lovely big village"; a commemorative book called it a "river of concrete and glass." In contrast to the rough textures of British estates, it appears as pristine as one would expect in a region celebrated for watchmaking. The rigorous geometry of the curtain wall is varied by the random distribution of yellow, red, and blue blinds, which residents select from the palette approved by the architects.

The Cité du Lignon is a highly successful realization of Corbu's vision of a Ville Radieuse, occupying only 8 percent of the site and being an almost self-sufficient community, with two pools atop the taller tower, a medical center, a school, two churches, shopping, and facilities for sports, youth, and seniors. Underground garages and bus stops eliminate the clutter of surface parking. A quarter of the apartments are subsidized; others are occupied by professionals who work nearby at CERN (the European Centre for Nuclear Research). An award-winning, three-year study to conserve the fabric and reduce energy consumption was begun in 2008. Architect Franz Graf developed strategies for updating the insulation without compromising the appearance of this listed building.

Le Corbusier sowed the seed of modernism in South America on trips he made there around 1930, and it flowered extravagantly in the following decades. His Brazilian protégé, Oscar Niemeyer, developed a distinctive language of sensually curved forms, inspired by his love of the female body. From the buildings he created around Lake Pampulha in the early 1940s, he progressed to the monumental structures of Brasília. Along the way, he designed several apartment blocks—most ambitiously the 1,000-unit Edifício Copan in

The brick towers of Rogelio Salmona's Torres del Parque (1964–70) rise
from a park near the center of Bogotá, and overlook a bullring.

Park Hill (1955–60), a brutalist complex of 1,000 apartments, was designed by the city architects of Sheffield and is now undergoing a major renovation.

Cité du Lignon (1963–71) was built to house 10,000 residents on the outskirts of Geneva. As refined as Park Hill (left) is rugged, it is a flourishing, well-serviced community.

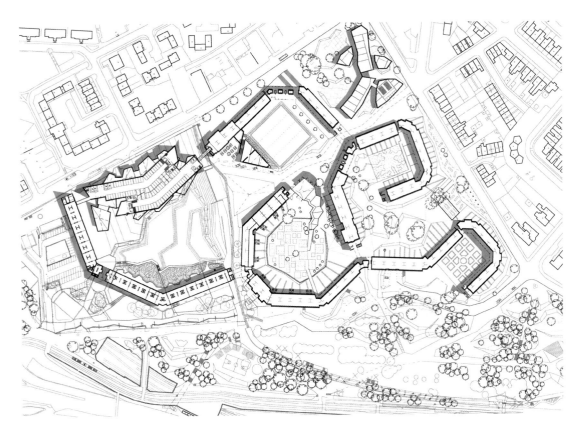

Site plan of Park Hill in Sheffield (above, left).

São Paulo. As that vast block was taking shape, he completed the Edifício Liberdade (1954–60), a luxury apartment building in the provincial city of Belo Horizonte that was later renamed Edifício Niemeyer in honor of Oscar's brother, Paulo. The biomorphism of the plan recalls Mies van der Rohe's unrealized glass skyscraper of 1922. But its voluptuousness, balance of horizontality and verticality, and thin sun breaks— three per floor—give it an entirely different character. Solid walls are clad in spotted cement tiles, adding another layer of richness. A lifelong communist, who went into exile when the military seized power in 1964, Niemeyer was always willing to house the *haute bourgeoisie* in style.

Colombia lacked the resources of Brazil, but it produced a great architect in Rogelio Salmona. His first major project was the Torres del Parque (1964–70), a masterly complex of three brick-clad apartment towers and a park at the heart of Bogotá. It may have been his response to Corbu's iconoclastic and unrealized proposal for a Unité block in the capital, a project on which Salmona collaborated. Rising from a podium and overlooking a Moorish-style bullring, the towers have curved profiles and balconies that project out at different angles and are wonderfully urbane. The interweaving of private and public space adds to its appeal, and Salmona lived there until his death in 2007. The duplex apartments were ingeniously planned and inexpensive, but they were broken up into small rooms for working-class families—who preferred to live in houses that could be easily extended. Sales were sparse for many years; today, the city's intellectual elite pay a premium to live there, and several apartments have been inventively remodeled by architect Felipe Uribe.

It is always a good sign when an architect chooses to live in one of his own creations, and Moshe Safdie was briefly a resident of Habitat 67, the prefabricated apartment building he created for Expo 67 in Montreal. For nine months, Safdie held court in his dream project as visitors streamed through and the waterfront surged with activity. "And yet with all those millions of people, when you closed the door, you were in your own house," he recalled, "on the tenth floor, in an environment that had ten times the density of [a suburb]."

Despite official funding, it was a huge struggle to get Habitat built, and it provoked fierce opposition. The design evolved from Safdie's graduate thesis; he had built nothing at that point. August Komendant, a visionary engineer, figured out how to make it work, by stacking load-bearing concrete units rather than employing a plug-in frame. The Canadian government abruptly halved the budget, forcing a reduction in the number of one- to four-module apartments from 950 to 158, greatly increasing the per-unit cost.

As Safdie recounts in his book on the project, "Habitat had . . . to challenge industry, the practice of labor, the by-laws, and the state of building art of the time . . . The design cost—two million dollars—was building research. [In fact] the whole cost of design and construction, twenty million dollars, should be considered research." Concrete was too heavy to be an ideal choice, but plastics were untested. Safdie discovered that the building industry is too fragmented to research new materials and uses only what is currently available—in contrast to most manufacturers. Despite the setbacks and compromises, Habitat has fulfilled its primary goal: to create a richly varied living environment from repetitive units. Fifty years on, it is owned by its residents and has become a green oasis with a long waiting list for prospective buyers. Safdie is restoring the unit he still owns and plans to gift it to a non-profit to open for public tours.

No such luck attended the Nagakin Capsule Tower, a radical exercise in prefabrication completed in Tokyo in 1972, which has deteriorated badly and is now threatened

Patrick Hodgkinson designed the Brunswick Centre as a counterpoint to the Georgian terraces of London's Bloomsbury district. Partially completed in 1972, it was recently refurbished by two of his former associates.

with demolition. It was an era of visionary schemes, from the avant-garde concepts of Archigram in Britain and Superstudio in Italy to the plug-in megastructures that Paul Rudolph designed for Manhattan. Those projects remained on paper, as did Kenzo Tange's proposal to extend Tokyo across its bay. Kisho Kurokawa, however, realized his design for a tower in which 144 residential capsules are bolted to two reinforced-concrete shafts containing stairs and elevators, rising from a two-story podium. Each capsule is the size of a shipping container and is fully equipped for a single resident.

The tower, now almost as shabby and neglected as Moisei Ginzburg's Narkomfin in Moscow (an idealistic exercise in communal living), is a rare survivor of the short-lived Metabolist movement. It was intended as a prototype for a mobile urban society. Kurokawa imagined a world in which residents would transport their customized capsules from one location to another and have them craned into supporting frames, as though they were docking a small boat.

The Brunswick Centre is one of the more sympathetic additions to the Georgian enclave of Bloomsbury in central London. Patrick Hodgkinson finalized the ziggurat design in 1965 after securing a promise from London County Council (LCC) that the entire scheme would be built privately as a mixed-use development with a density of 200 people per acre (0.4 ha) within an 80 ft (24 m) height limit. As he explained, "It was to be a village, not a megastructure, and never brutalist, but rather would create a poetic construct of feel and not look."

Two parallel five-story blocks containing about 400 apartments rise from a podium of parking and enclose a shopping mall. An opening in the north block frames the tree-filled square beyond. Responsibility passed from the LCC to Camden Borough Council and to McAlpine's, a large

Habitat 67 was Moshe Safdie's bold experiment in creating a vibrant community from repetitive units. Located in Montreal, overlooking the St. Lawrence River, it was a celebrated exhibit of Expo 67 and has become a highly desirable place to live.

construction company that had little interest in housing. As Hodgkinson tells the story, the builder failed to finish the scheme as designed, to paint or face the concrete, to build the glass-covered shopping hall, or to enclose the top-level housing access-way.

Completed in 1972, the Brunswick Centre went into decline until it was listed in 2000 and Levitt Bernstein, a firm established by two former associates of Hodgkinson, began to rehabilitate the exteriors. Their efforts have turned a bedraggled relic into a showcase of prosperity, with upscale retail and an art cinema. Camden belatedly upgraded rental

apartments and waterproofed the balconies. The common areas have become scruffy, but the diverse mix of owners, seniors, and council tenants is deeply attached to the property. "I've lived here for ten years and consider it an incredibly successful development with lots of social interaction," says architect David Levitt.

Piet Blom explored the idea of placing a cube on one of its corners in several Dutch cities before realizing Blaak Heights Cube Houses (1978–84), his most ambitious project, in Rotterdam. The tight-knit complex of 100 units is clustered around a raised courtyard and accessed from a switchback

Nemausus (1985–87) comprises two parallel blocks of prefabricated apartments on a concrete frame. It was designed by Jean Nouvel as a commission from the progressive mayor of Nîmes, France.

The cube houses and pencil-shaped apartment tower at Blaak Heights in Rotterdam, an innovative project of Piet Blom, were completed in 1984.

The Nagakin Capsule Tower in Tokyo was a visionary Metabolist project of Kisho Kurokawa. Completed in 1972 and now decrepit, its future is uncertain.

Foster + Partners designed the Chesa Futura apartments (2000–03) on a site overlooking St. Moritz. The flattened sphere is clad in larch shingles.

ramp. The cubes straddle a busy road and lean in protectively like medieval gables, providing shelter from persistent wind and rain, and shade on sunny days. Yellow cladding panels add a cheerful note. The three-level cubes are snug, and the sloping walls and peaked glass vault impart a dynamism that compensates to some degree for the lack of square footage. Smaller units are grouped in a polygonal fourteen-story tower whose sharply pointed roof caused it to be dubbed the Pencil. The cubes come on the market at moderate prices, and one is open to the public as a museum.

Nemausus was the Roman name for Nîmes, a city in the South of France. It is also the name given to the radical social housing project that Jean Nouvel built there between 1985 and 1987 at the invitation of Jean Bousquet, a progressive mayor. Their goal was to create spacious, flexible, and affordable apartments, ranging from studios to triplexes, in two long blocks running east–west. To hold down rents, Nouvel specified prefabricated components that were easy to assemble: sheet aluminum and metal mesh on a poured concrete frame. Exterior staircases, flared guardrails, and a rooftop canopy have an industrial character, softened by the plane trees that separate the blocks, which are raised above the ground on pilotis. Each of the 114 apartments has a double exposure to facilitate cross-ventilation, and concertina doors open onto the 10 ft (3 m) wide access decks that surround the blocks on three levels. Those projecting elements give the blocks the look of beached cruise ships, looming over a neighborhood of tiled-roof cottages and workshops.

It is said that the Swiss subsidize the price of milk to ensure that cows continue grazing on Alpine meadows, and

Contemporaine (2001–04) is an apartment tower by Perkins + Will that builds on Chicago's long tradition of inventive high-rise buildings.

rural areas are deeply conservative when it comes to any variations on the traditional wooden chalet. Contextualism rules, but Foster + Partners skilfully negotiated a bold departure from the norm in St. Moritz. Chesa Futura (House of the Future, 2000–03) is a slightly flattened sphere containing three stories of apartments, raised on eight steel pilotis above two levels of underground parking. It is a prefabricated timber building designed as a demonstration of economy, in its sustainability and modest footprint. Although the form is novel, the larch shingles echo the vernacular, will turn silver, and should last for a hundred years. Nestled among other buildings on a rise overlooking the town, it has broad sheltered decks that open up to the south, framing mountain views; the north side, meanwhile, is protected, with deep-set windows.

In Chicago, successive generations of architects have advanced the art of building, creating a timeless and enduring legacy, and Perkins + Will—a firm best known for its work in education and healthcare—has made an important contribution to the stock of multiple housing. Contemporaine (2001–04) is a modestly scaled apartment tower on a confined site at the edge of downtown. Design director Ralph Johnson accepted the commission from a developer who—in contrast to so many of his profession—had a strong appreciation of architecture and was willing to spend what it took to achieve a building of rare distinction.

A glazed podium contains street-level retail and three levels of parking, which are linked by an exposed ramp. There are nine stories of apartments, plus four interlocking penthouses with double- or triple-height living rooms at the top. Concrete is used consistently throughout, and the massing of the building owes a debt to Corbu, even to the Russian Constructivists. The corner entry is cut away to a height of four stories, and this lofty void is echoed in a hood that crowns the tower, with a single slender column supporting both corners. Balconies are alternately recessed and boldly cantilevered. The dramatic interplay of mass and void, concrete and glass, gives this tower a stronger presence than conventional towers five times as high.

Each of these projects offers valuable lessons in the creation of good living environments. The priorities include well-proportioned interiors with abundant natural light, well insulated to reduce energy consumption and keep noise at bay. Ideally, they should enjoy views and cross-ventilation. A balance of privacy and sociability turns proximity to advantage. Residential blocks should be mixed-use so that different activities can mingle. Ground-floor stores stimulate street life and raise apartments above the traffic flow. Plantings provide shade, absorb carbon dioxide, and mediate between the interior and the city. Huge complexes can be humane places for a wide variety of residents, as long as they are well built and maintained, provided with essential services and connections, and softened by generous plantings. The Cité du Lignon is a prime example that has been sensitively updated; Park Hill was neglected but has been radically upgraded and is enjoying a new lease of life.

Although it is good to break out of the box, adding amenities and greenery, it is the interiors that count for the most. The high-ceilinged prewar apartments in the blocks around New York's Central Park are among the most desirable places to live, though their façades are often unremarkable. They achieve a level of quality that has become increasingly rare, and their generous spaces are best matched in loft conversions. Adaptive reuse is an ideal way of renewing a city's heritage, but that is a topic for another book. Contemporary architects have different strategies. Here, then, are thirty ground-up buildings that strive for originality and excellence.

URBAN VILLAGES

The village is the ur-community: a basic unit of human habitation that grows organically from the land its inhabitants cultivate. It can be idyllic or oppressive—often both together; it might be picture-perfect or a squalid backwater. People flee villages in search of opportunity in big cities, where a few prosper and the majority struggle for advancement. The villages of emerging countries may eventually shrivel, as they have in the West, leaving a few to be rehabilitated as tourist showcases. Although the village is an archaic model, its tight-knit social network and human scale have inspired architects to channel its spirit in urban developments.

Every multiple housing project, of whatever size, challenges the designer to balance privacy and interaction, openness and protection, giving every resident a sense of possession and community, within both the building and the neighborhood. That can be easier to achieve on a small scale, as in a village, where the development hugs the ground or embraces nature, and where everyone knows their neighbors. The best of these projects combine the convenience of apartment living with the complexity of a house, fusing the individual and the collective in a satisfying whole.

This ideal can be achieved in many ways. On the bleak Castilian plain at the edge of Madrid, Morphosis reinterpreted the gleaming white casbahs of Algeria and Tunisia, in part to house a new wave of immigrants who may have been familiar with that model. The individual units are subsumed within a single complex threaded through with shaded walkways and patios. In the ancient city of Kyoto, Kazuyo Sejima brought her delicate touch to a cluster of ten units shaded by tilted roofs that resembles a traditional village from above. Below, they have a lightness and transparency that is entirely contemporary in feeling, and engenders a sense of intimacy that is peculiarly Japanese. Only in a culture where people are used to making the most of small spaces and living in close proximity to one another could such a development as this prove a comfortable fit.

An adaptive reuse project in the Slovenian capital of Ljubljana comes closest to realizing the privacy–community ideal. OFIS rehabilitated a linked trio of baroque houses, restoring the outer walls and roofs and excavating a cluttered courtyard. The historical fabric was sheathed in glass to pull natural light into three levels of apartments, and the reflections serve as a privacy screen. In a former industrial area of Turin, Luciano Pia turned a larch-shingled block into a virtual tree house, framing densely planted balconies with Corten-steel tree trunks that mimic the real trees in the courtyard. Boréal is a block of social housing in a depressed suburb of Nantes, where Tetrarc layered a plain stucco block with fully glazed winter gardens that look out to allotments and woods, and provided upper-level access to the rear from a fanciful construction of wood staves. Finally, in the Southern California city of Santa Monica, Kevin Daly linked four blocks with elevated walkways that serve as social generators and frame a landscaped courtyard.

CARABANCHEL HOUSING: HISPANIC CASBAH

Calle Patrimonio de la Humanidad No. 1, Carabanchel, Madrid

Morphosis
2002–07

On the eve of the Spanish housing crash, which left swathes of speculative construction standing empty, Morphosis completed a competition-winning social housing project in Carabanchel, a master-planned community bordered by the ring road to the southwest of Madrid. A gleaming white complex of cubist blocks, patios, and walkways, it evokes the hill villages of Andalusia or the casbahs of North Africa. It is one of twenty-seven projects in the area sponsored by EMVS, the city housing authority. These were all designed by young or established architects, from Spain and abroad, and are scattered among the bland brick middle-class apartment blocks, privately developed for a market that no longer exists.

All these blocks have been plopped down on the edge of the bleak Castilian plain, offering no sense of place or incentive to live so far from the vibrant city center. However, the land was cheap and social housing is always in demand, allowing the completed units to be offered for sale or rent at a third of the market rate.

The construction budget was a frugal 600 euros per sq m (11 sq ft), but Morphosis principal Thom Mayne rose to the challenge: "We've always made a practice of building inexpensively," he says. "I share the idealism of the early modernists, and the client gave us free rein conceptually as long as we met the budget." For this, its first venture in Spain, Mayne's team collaborated with BDU Estudio de Arquitectura, a fledgling Madrid firm founded by Begoña Díaz-Urgorri, who briefly worked for Morphosis and gained experience building another innovative project for EMVS.

In 2007, at the height of the boom, 900,000 housing units were built in Spain—almost as many as were constructed in the rest of Europe. This was due partly to a surge of immigration, partly to a frenzy of speculation, but most of the privately financed houses and apartment blocks were conventional in design and poorly constructed. The public housing is much more adventurous, and Mayne's vision, which was fleshed out by Díaz-Urgorri and Morphosis project architect Pavel Getov, is a brilliant reworking of the Mediterranean vernacular. For immigrants from North Africa and the Middle East, this is a home away from home: tight-knit, human in scale, a place to rebuild lives and community.

The architects stacked the two-bedroom apartments in a thin-section seven-story slab that runs along the north side of the site. The street façade has small openings, and the apartments open onto south-facing terraces at each level. A four-story block defines the south boundary, and these two bars of small units bracket a village-like complex of three- and four-bedroom duplexes, with a podium of parking below. A broad *paseo* (public walk), shaded by aluminum mesh canopies that support a variety of flowering plants, bisects the complex from north to south, connecting to a network of narrow passages. Public plazas alternate with inner patios. "We tried to create an infrastructure for social interchange, with neighbors meeting casually and conversing from one space to another," says Mayne.

To keep construction costs down, the architects produced variations on a simple, three-dimensional module, and employed the standard building system of a concrete structural frame and stuccoed brick infill. Mesh-covered Styrofoam panels sprayed with cement are supported on steel poles to define the *paseo*. The mature trees that Morphosis had wanted to plant were eliminated as an economy, and the plantings have yet to soften the canopies, giving the project a sharp-edged Constructivist look. The 141 two-, three-, and four-bedroom units are compact (600–1,000 sq ft/56–93 sq m) but attractively finished, with hardwood floors, terrazzo stairs, and built-in cabinets. Chimney-like towers serve as ventilation shafts, pulling in cool breezes and evacuating hot air, and natural ventilation from the open spaces keeps the units cool on all but the hottest days. Solar panels contribute to the heating, and abundant natural light also reduces energy costs.

For Morphosis, this project was a departure from the daring geometries of their public and institutional buildings. Here, for reasons of cost and practicality, they have created a multilayered complex from the simplest of building blocks, relying on bright sunlight to animate the spaces between the buildings. It is as though a virtuoso pianist were to turn from Bartók and Shostakovich, and play a simple melody with deep feeling.

A tight-knit complex of white apartments, reminiscent of North African casbahs, is located in the planned community of Carabanchel on the southwest edge of Madrid.

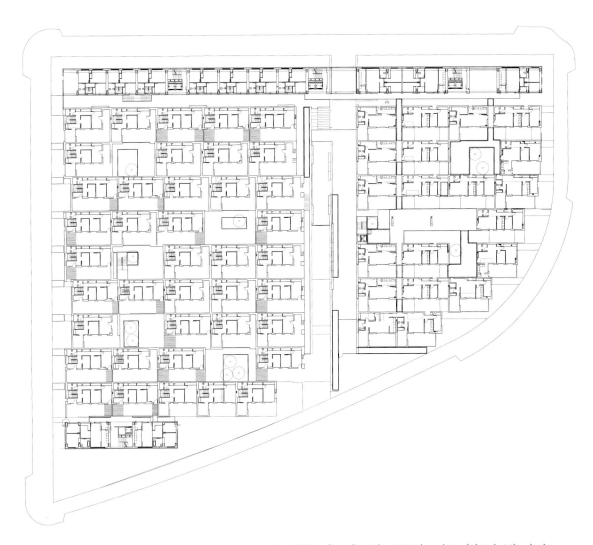

Opposite: Taller blocks of smaller units to north and south bracket the duplex apartments, which are closely grouped around plazas, patios, and walkways. This page: Sample floor plan and section.

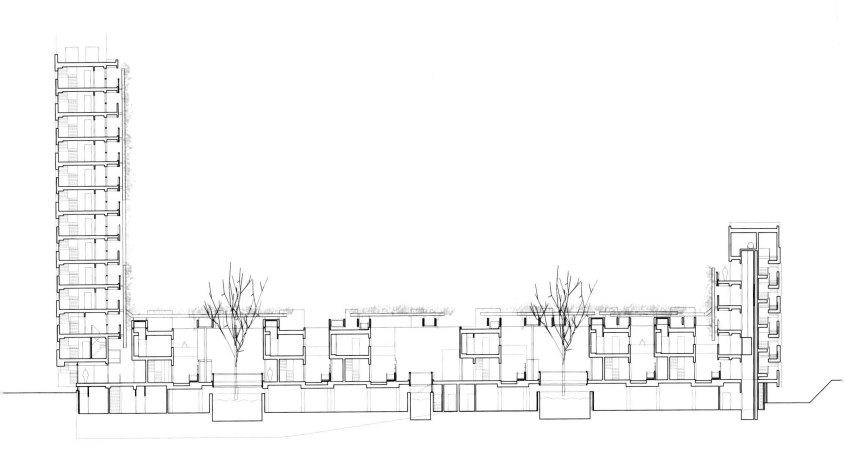

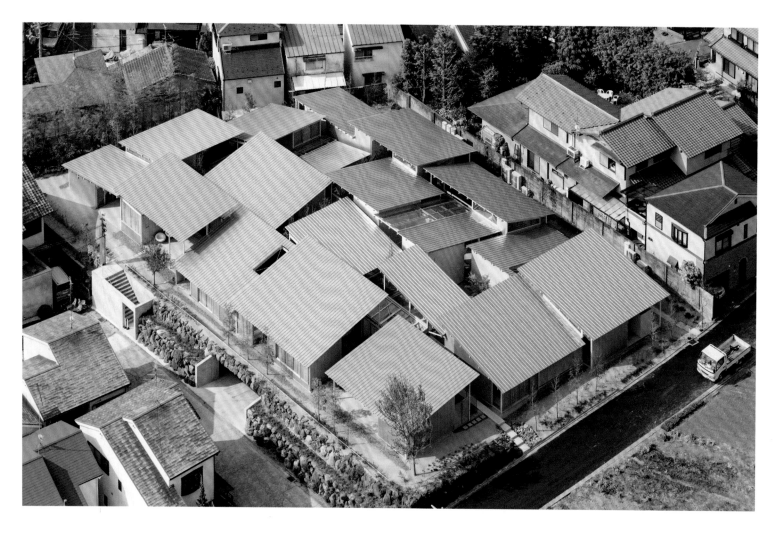

Nineteen shed roofs shade a dense cluster of ten apartments opening on to patios and walkways (opposite) in a northwestern suburb of Kyoto.

NISHINOYAMA HOUSE: DISSOLVING BOUNDARIES

Ukyo-ku, Kyoto-shi, Kyoto-fu 601-0316

Kazuyo Sejima & Associates
2010–13

Kyoto was the imperial capital of Japan until the relocation of the emperor and his court to Tokyo in 1869. Famed for its temples and gardens, Kyoto was spared Allied bombing in the Second World War, but much of the center and many of the old quarters have been ruthlessly redeveloped in recent decades. It is an odd paradox that the Japanese are both protective and destructive of their history, and new building is minutely regulated even as characterful neighborhoods and significant landmarks are swept away. The banality of many Japanese cities is relieved only by a scatter of historic fragments and new architect-designed buildings—often of great audacity—that are acclaimed worldwide. Nishinoyama

House, a complex of ten apartments located in a northwestern suburb of Kyoto, is one of these unexpected delights.

It was designed by Kazuyo Sejima, co-principal with Ryue Nishizawa of SANAA, who together won the Pritzker Prize in 2010 and joined the pantheon of Japanese architects who have made their mark at home and abroad. The partners work collaboratively and separately; here, Sejima was invited by the Hase Building Group to put ten housing units on a gently sloping corner site of 19,030 sq ft (1,770 sq m). That was the only requirement, and it gave the architect freedom to create a unique living environment that is woven into the neighborhood of single-family homes, and opens up to distant views of the city and Mount Hiei. Apartments vary in size from 590 to 1,080 sq ft (55 to 100 sq m), and each has a basement or loft.

A retaining wall of massive rocks conceals the parking level, and steps lead up from the street to narrow walkways that link the units, with their private decks, and the communal space where neighbors gather to party together. The levels shift in response to the topography of the site, which further enriches the spatial complexity and feeling of discovery as one moves through. Nishinoyama House has all the character of a village, with unexpected turns and a new composition around every corner. It also evokes the traditional tight-knit urban plan of Kyoto. Glass sliders dissolve the boundary between indoors and outdoors, much like the shoji screens in a traditional Japanese house, and the whole complex has the lightness and transparency that characterize nearly all of Sejima's work. Those are qualities that achieve a high point of development in Grace Farms, a foundation-funded project in New Canaan, Connecticut, which offers the public a pastoral idyll in an undulating sequence of glass-enclosed spaces.

The key feature of Nishinoyama House is the roofscape. As Sejima explains, "By regulation the roof must be sloped,

Large expanses of glass make the spacious apartments seem even larger, as do the private patios and semi-public walkways.

and initially we designed one big canopy, but that made the building appear too much like a commercial property. So we experimented with a roof on each room or each unit and ended with nineteen corrugated metal roofs that tilt up to admit natural light and air, while framing small inner gardens." Each unit has three roofs, one of which is shared with a neighbor. There are also three flat glass roofs at the center to pull in more light. The steel-framed structure meets the tough seismic code with a minimum of shear walls.

Although the apartments feel spacious, they are packed together more tightly and are more open to the inner walkways than in comparable developments in Europe and North America. Traditionally, most Japanese are frugal in their living patterns, cherishing tiny spaces that stand in for gardens or vistas. Each room serves different functions and there is a greater sense of communality than in the West. Sejima strove to achieve a balance of public, semi-public, and private space, and it helps that the residents are artists and other creatives, or *gaijin* (foreigners) seeking an authentically Japanese experience. Here, centuries of tradition are distilled into an immaterial structure that embraces nature and draws it inside. Every room catches shafts of sunlight, a fresh breeze, or a glimpse of a flowering tree.

Living in a glass house imposes a certain discipline, and the apartments tend to be sparely furnished with an eclectic mix of Western and Japanese pieces. There were no blinds on the windows initially, but the architects offered to install them on request. Floors are polished concrete or birch, with a tatami room for traditionalists; ceilings are white luan wood. Bathrooms are located to the rear of each unit, facing the private gardens.

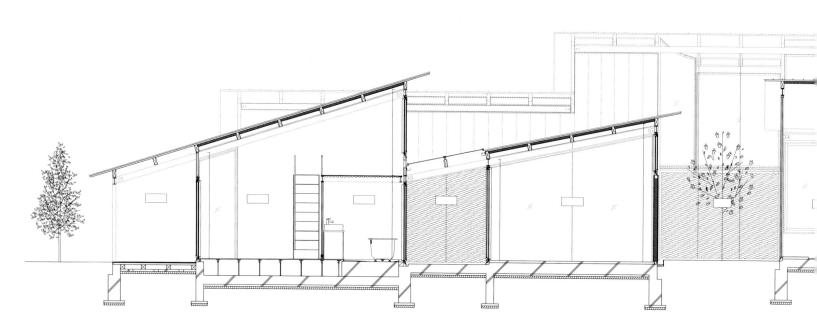

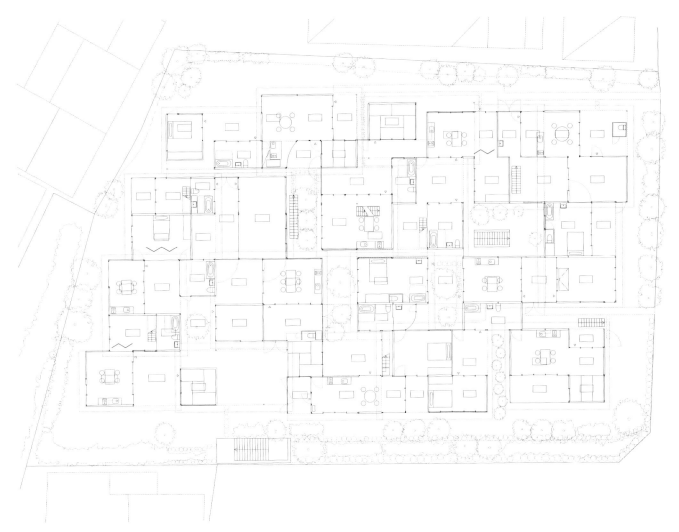

Opposite, top: A retaining wall of massive rocks conceals the parking level, which serves as a podium for the ten varied apartments. Above and below: Sample floor plan and section.

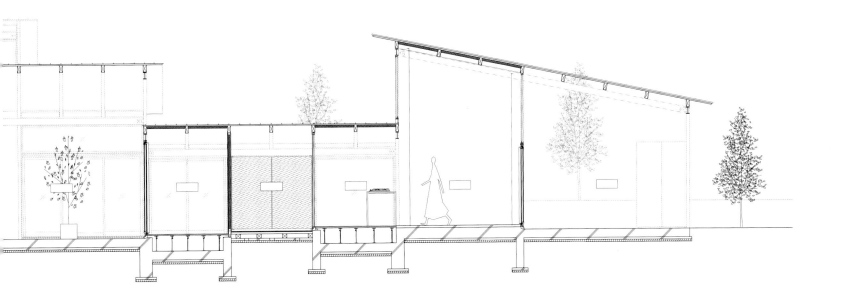

In the historic core of Ljubljana, the façades of three baroque houses were restored, and twelve apartments were created around a central courtyard.

BAROQUE COURT APARTMENTS: INTERNAL TRANSFORMATION

Stritarjeva ulica 3, Ljubljana

OFIS Arhitekti
2007–12

Slovenia was a province of the Austro-Hungarian Empire in 1895, when the capital, Ljubljana, was devastated by an earthquake. Much of it was rebuilt in the Secession style that was then fashionable in Vienna, but older structures were restored. Today, the city is a historical palimpsest, enlivened by the idiosyncratic buildings of Jože Plečnik, the Gaudí of Ljubljana. The local firm of OFIS, a partnership of Rok Oman and Spela Videčnik, made its reputation with historical restoration—notably of the City Museum. That project made the firm a natural choice for a publishing company that wanted to relocate its offices from a trio of baroque houses, while keeping its street-level bookstore, and turn the four upper floors into a complex of twelve apartments.

The Baroque Court Apartments are located at the heart of the old town, next to City Hall and close to Plečnik's three bridges. There, in the historic core, the authorities keep a watchful eye on exteriors, requiring that street façades and the tiled roofs that are visible from the castle should conform to tradition. OFIS refaced the century-old stucco façades in the language of the baroque with stone-framed openings, but

Above, below right, and opposite: Expansive glazing blurs the boundary between shared and private space. Below: The project's location in Ljubljana.

were left to themselves in remodeling the interiors. Videčnik observes: "Because the houses were small, they shared a linear courtyard, but this had been filled in, with storage below and meeting rooms above, so we created a new landscaped courtyard atop the storage. We were peeling away the postwar additions and then discovered stone columns and arches from the original construction, which survived the 1895 earthquake and had been enclosed." She speculates that fragments of the building may date back to the Gothic era, given its proximity to the castle looming above.

Accorded a free hand and a budget of 2.5 million euros, OFIS decided to keep anything that seemed significant and then to enclose the excavated elements in double glazing. This forms a transparent membrane that puts the arched columns into a vitrine and extends the apartments (like the winter gardens of Boréal, page 55), while blurring the boundary between private and shared space. The glass also pulls in the reflections of surrounding buildings, which adds a layer of privacy during the day. The apartments that face the courtyard can be screened off with heavy curtains—though they are surprisingly little used. In this tight-knit community people get used to living in a goldfish bowl.

From the courtyard the castle is clearly visible, but from above the glazing dissolves into the jumble of tiled roofs, and

there the architects had to limit themselves to the traditional small openings. The entry lobby and storerooms for each resident share the ground floor with the bookshop. There are four apartments, ranging in size from 750 to 1,500 sq ft (70 to 140 sq m), on each of three floors, with mezzanine galleries for sleeping or additional storage. The third level contains duplexes, with the upper level tucked into the pitch of the roof. Residents—including several Russian families who find Ljubljana a congenial escape from their often turbulent homeland—pay a premium for the distinctive character and location of these spacious apartments, and appreciate the seismic reinforcement that came with the remodel. One family moved from a house on the outskirts of the city into a much smaller space in order to be near the center. Inflation drove up prices initially but, as the recession took hold, they were then discounted. Baroque Court is a model of adaptive reuse, although, as Videčnik notes, "It's very rare for an entire building in the historic center to have a single owner, so there have been no similar conversions."

One recent OFIS project is a prefabricated alpine shelter, developed in collaboration with students at Harvard Graduate School of Design, with three sections lifted to the site by helicopter. The firm recently enhanced its reputation for conservation by creating a dramatic living space within a traditional barn that was threatened with demolition, like so many instances of the rural vernacular. The architects have also built many examples of social housing in and around Ljubljana, trying to give each apartment a separate identity within repetitive prefabricated structures; one project comprised 650 units, which had to be built in two years. The architects realized that a layer of balconies, loggias, and bay windows would give the buildings an added depth, and would be used intensively in this Mediterranean climate. However, to their regret, they have found that nearly all their clients—both public and private —are concerned principally with costs and have little interest in architecture.

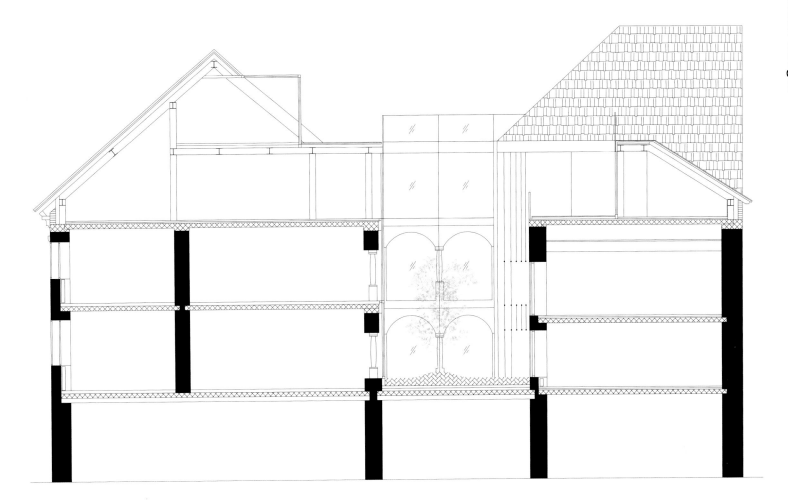

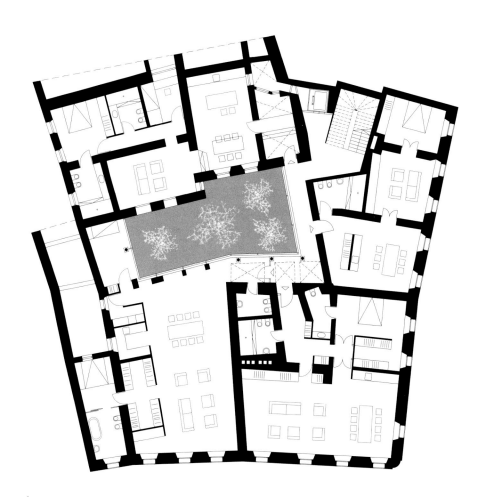

Opposite: Four apartments on each floor share a view of the landscaped courtyard, while the upper-level duplexes have an attic story that offers glimpses over the roofs of the old town. This page: Section and sample floor plan.

In remodeling the old houses, the architects excavated the remnants of different eras and made them part of their design, as seen in the vaulted ceiling of the bathroom (opposite) and the columns and arches of the living area (below).

25 VERDE: CORTEN FOREST

Via Chiabrera 25, Turin

Luciano Pia
2007–13

Stately baroque squares and automobile factories are two of the contradictory ingredients of Italy's most progressive city. Turin was laid out by the Romans, flourished for centuries as the seat of the dukes of Savoy, and briefly served (1861–64) as the first capital of a united Italy. Le Corbusier praised its location, sandwiched between the Alps and the Po River, as the most beautiful of any city in Europe. It abounds in surprises, the most recent of which is a green apartment complex that seems to be growing out of a former industrial zone, like a tree taking root in an abandoned factory.

25 Verde is the first ground-up apartment block by Luciano Pia, an architect who worked in Paris in the 1990s and opened his office in Turin in 2000. Prior to this, he restored and converted old structures and designed offices and a hotel; the University of Turin's Molecular Biotechnology Center is a study in reticence. Getting anything built in Italy can be a struggle—particularly a work of great originality—but Pia was fortunate in having a site that is well removed from the historic center, across the street from one of Fiat's first workshops, and a developer who was open to doing something new. It comprises a six-story, U-plan block that encloses a densely planted garden, with a partly open ground floor and two levels of parking below. The concrete-frame structure has a peripheral frame of tree skeletons laser-cut from Corten, a material that refers to the industrial past.

The steel helps to support broad terraces around the perimeter and the planters for 150 trees, putting each of the sixty-three apartments in the midst of nature, front and back. The garden is a place for everyone to meet; the terraces extend the living areas. Footbridges traverse a pond, and the private roof terraces are also lushly planted. Sunlight filters between the wood planks of the terraces, which double as a

brise-soleil. There are views out to mountains and green hills. Residents who might have driven to the country at weekends now stay home in their own little piece of the *campagna*.

The jagged edges of the steel trees and the exposed frame that supports them are softened by the greenery and by the larch shingles that clad the walls. The Corten is as tactile as tree bark, and seems more organic than a manufactured product. The whole building has an irregular, handmade character that provides a welcome oasis for the neighborhood, in contrast to Stefano Boeri's Bosco Verticale in Milan, a conventional tower in which trees in planters are lofted high above the street and have little value for pedestrians. At 25 Verde, natural and man-made elements are intricately woven together. Residents are deeply devoted to the plantings, maintaining their own balconies with help from the gardeners who tend the courtyard. Plant experts advised on the choice of species, which are native to Piedmont or easily adapt to local conditions. There is a diversity of leaves, colors, and flowering cycles. Some are evergreen, but most are deciduous, shedding leaves in winter to admit sun and light. In addition to providing shade and creating a microclimate within, the trees produce oxygen, absorb carbon dioxide, reduce air pollution, and cut noise. They are irrigated with recycled rainwater, and the building is heated and cooled with geothermal energy.

Here, as in all his work, Pia puts a strong emphasis on the spirit of place, opening buildings up to nature, conserving energy, and expressing the natural character of materials. It has become fashionable to talk of green architecture and emphasize one's commitment to sustainability. Pia, like Édouard François in Paris, practices what he preaches. The Corten and plantings added little to the cost of construction, and the apartments—which range in size from 480 to 1,720 sq ft (45 to 160 sq m)—have attracted a diversity of middle-income residents, including professionals who work at home. Pia created varied open plans that can be divided up to suit different patterns of living—spaces that seem to change their character through the day and with the seasons.

Skeletal Corten "trees" help to support broad decks and steel planters, making the entire complex an extension of the wooded courtyard.

Lush greenery throughout the site softens the angular structure and complements the soft-toned larch shingles.

This page: Broad wooden decks extend the living spaces of all the apartments and provide shade in summer. Opposite: Sample floor plan and section.

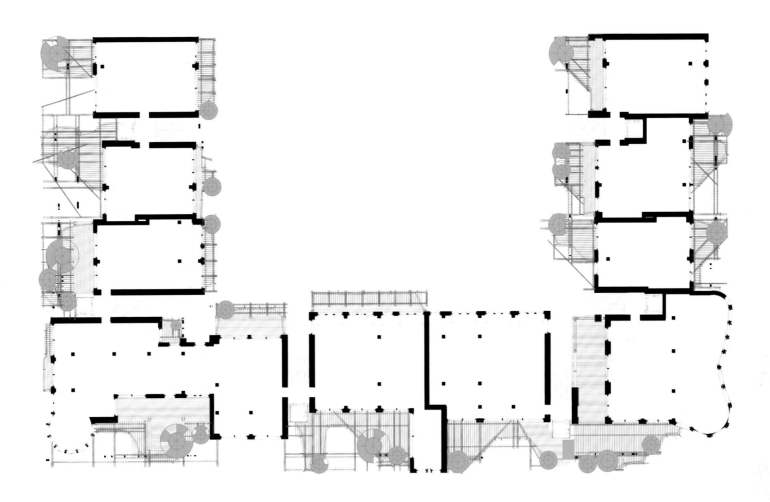

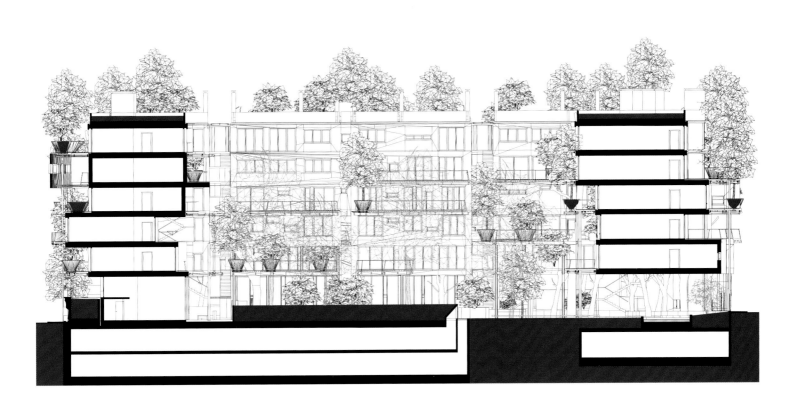

BORÉAL: EMBRACING NATURE

Rue Auguste Lepère 4, Dervallières, Nantes

Tetrarc
2007–11

Nantes, a port city near the Atlantic coast of France, recovered from the devastation of war to become one of the most vibrant of provincial centers. But, as in Paris and other French cities, social housing was pushed to the outer edge, where the poor were warehoused in such concrete barracks as the vast Sillon de Bretagne. One of the new suburbs is Dervallières, which is officially classified as a Sensitive Urban Zone, with high unemployment, few high-school graduates, and a low level of home ownership. The government-funded National Agency for Urban Renewal is trying to revitalize this depressed neighborhood by upgrading the housing stock and increasing the amount of green space. Tetrarc, a lively local architectural firm, was commissioned to create a new model of affordable living.

Boréal—a play on the word *arboreal*—is a five-story block of social housing that takes its cues from nature. It replaces an unsightly 1960s tower block and represents a fresh start, combining sixteen spacious owner-occupied duplexes with twenty-three smaller rental units and knitting them together with allotments and the forest beyond. The apartments range in size from 540 to 960 sq ft (50 to 90 sq m), and are grouped in eleven linked bays, each set at a 21-degree angle to the next, so that they fan out like a hand of cards. To the southwest, the apartments open into fully glazed winter gardens that command sweeping views of the forested surroundings. These enclosures double the apparent size of the apartments, pull in abundant natural light, serve as thermal barriers, and mediate between indoors and out. Windows at top and bottom open to circulate fresh air. The apartments extend the full width of the block and are entered from the northeast side, where each of the eleven stucco façades is painted a different tone from the red end of the spectrum. This combines with the pitched roofs to suggest a row of townhouses, each with its own individuality.

The most distinctive feature of Boréal is the pair of free-standing wooden enclosures that provide access to the third and fourth levels. Like giant pergolas, constructed from staves and lofted on splayed supports, they evoke the stilt houses of the South Seas. Project directors Michel Bertreux and Daniel Caud claim they were inspired by beach cabins, the writings of Ralph Waldo Emerson, and, rather surprisingly, *Star Wars*. Whatever the source, this is an inspired addition that was inexpensive to construct and transforms the rear façade of the block. It creates a dramatic chiaroscuro on sunny days and provides a two-level deck on which neighbors can gather and socialize. It also serves as a point of access across bridges to the third and fourth levels, with stairs and elevators leading to the second and fifth levels. That eliminates internal corridors. Underground parking allows grass to flow up to the building.

Each of the thirty-nine units has its own allotment for growing vegetables and promoting a sense of community, and these are grouped together on the southwest side. The stave fences that separate them echo the wood structure to the

Double-height winter gardens to the south (left) admit the sun and enlarge the apartments, which are entered from the north side at ground level or from bridges that extend from wooden pergolas (below and opposite).

rear, and the pairs of garden huts mimic the roofline of the block. There is a sense of play—in the transparency, the warm colors, and the layering of space—that gives Boréal a strong sense of place. How rarely does any housing, especially when it is built on a modest budget for low-income families, emphasize the pleasure principle?

For Tetrarc, the success of Boréal has spurred its efforts to create more innovative housing projects, which currently include a modular prefabricated scheme, alongside commercial and institutional buildings that share the same quality of witty invention. The firm's own office, for example, is housed in Manny, a mixed-use block that is wrapped in metal bands. Close by, on the banks of the Loire, is La Fabrique, a fanciful tower of glass and metal, containing studios and offices that rise above a raw concrete bunker. More recent is Rives de Seine, twin blocks of social housing on Île Seguin, the former site of Renault factories in the Boulogne-Billancourt district of Paris. Tetrarc's signature metal ribbons are entwined around the projecting balconies that punctuate the larger block, creating a series of sinuous gazebos.

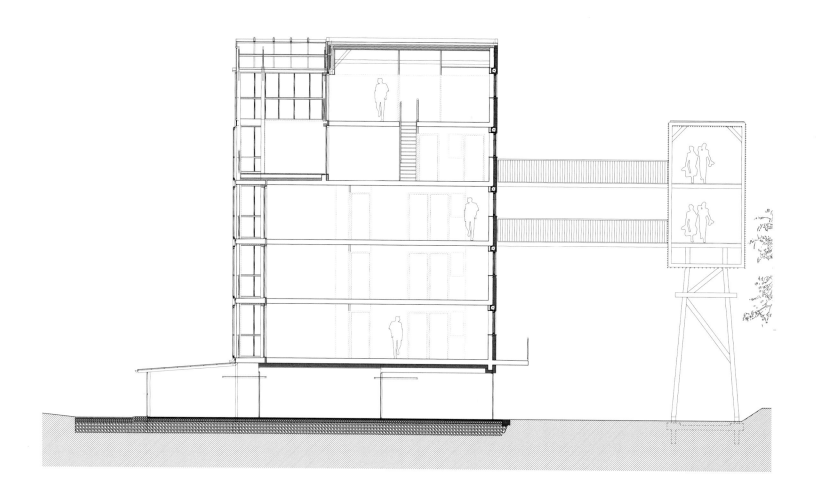

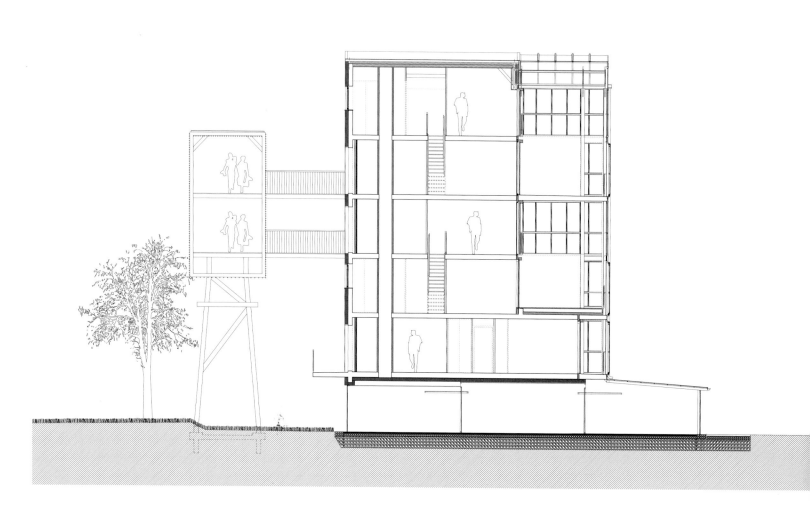

Above: The winter gardens have the character of an industrial loft and serve as indoor–outdoor living areas year-round. Opposite and below: Two sections and a sample floor plan.

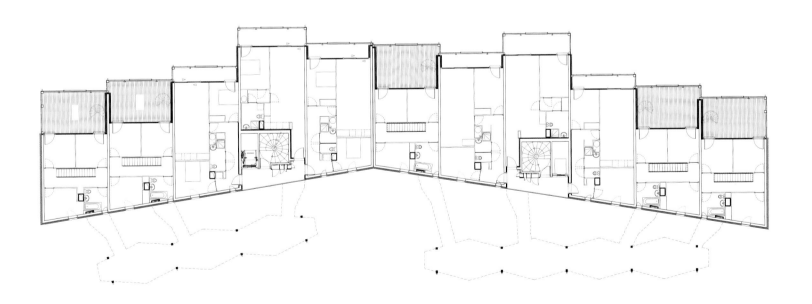

BROADWAY HOUSING: INTIMATE ENCLAVE

Broadway at 26th Street, Santa Monica, California

**Kevin Daly Architects
2009–12**

Santa Monica was once a sleepy seaside town, a weekend resort with a streetcar running to downtown Los Angeles. In the 1960s, a freeway replaced the streetcar, and the recent addition of a light-rail link has made it an even more desirable (and expensive) place to live and work. The Rand Corporation think tank has joined a host of media and tech start-ups, and there is a boom in new construction. Young couples can no longer afford a house, and even professionals are being priced out. And yet the progressive city government has done more than any other in Southern California to promote affordable housing, encouraging leading local architects to achieve a high level of design.

Kevin Daly is best known for his inventive private houses, but he recently completed two projects for the non-profit Community Corporation of Santa Monica (CCSM). Broadway Housing is located on a corner site that was formerly occupied by a nursing home, across the street from a large community park. Four three-story blocks are arranged in pinwheel fashion so they are not directly facing one another. To achieve a balance of privacy and openness, they are screened by wood battens and mature sycamores in the starfish-shaped courtyard—a strategy inspired by Daly's Laybourne house in the neighboring district of Venice. There, the main house and guest apartment over the garage face each other across a garden, and the expansive glazing is screened with perforated metal.

Broadway was tightly budgeted, but Daly was able to provide generous living spaces and give the frugal structure a strong sense of identity. Canted metal hoods shade sun-facing windows, and extend inside to create seating nooks. The other walls are inexpensively clad in brown or ice-blue Hardie board, which acts as a rain screen, allowing air to circulate to the stucco surface behind. The four blocks are connected by walkways at the two upper levels and (as in Boréal, page 55) these double as accessways and gathering places. In Southern California, where one can live outdoors for much of the year, these decks promote a sense of community, which is strengthened by the communal buildings for meetings and after-school activities, as well as a children's playground. Planters for the trees extend down into the underground parking.

There is a strong emphasis on sustainability, from the cross-ventilation that draws in ocean breezes to the shade of trees and the green roofs of the communal buildings. Rainwater—a precious commodity in this region—is collected on site and stored in an underground cistern, from which it is circulated for irrigation.

The thirty-three two- and three-bedroom apartments—810 and 1,050 sq ft (75 and 98 sq m)—are well proportioned and constructed, with abundant natural light. CCSM rents them to families earning 30–60 percent of the city's median income. In contrast to many social housing projects, there is no stigma attached to Broadway. As Daly observes, "My architect friends who walked through with me said they'd live

2602

there in a heartbeat, especially with the garden, and park across the street. People are looking for well-designed, efficient housing—not fancy countertops." Indeed, he sees greater opportunity for creative design in social housing than in upscale condos, where residents prioritize privacy over community. The CCSM believes it is better to eliminate the front gate and have residents be responsible for security. With 100 residents, including many children, it is safe to leave doors and windows open. Each gallery accesses only three apartments to promote a feeling of intimacy.

A hundred such projects are needed to meet the growing demand for affordable housing, but land is costly, available sites are few, and funding for housing associations is limited.

The city allows greater density when a project is affordable, but there is often opposition from the neighbors to anything that might lower property values or increase traffic—although Broadway quickly won acceptance for the quality of its design. Daly sees a need for financial incentives, and housing co-ops as an alternative to development companies. Small developers could do self-financed projects, sharing the appreciation in value over time with residents. Building regulations that delay construction and add to the cost should be relaxed. There also has to be greater use of innovative materials and technologies. Daly cites the student housing he is building in Santa Barbara, which employs a high level of prefabrication to save time and cost.

Opposite: Residents enjoy a community room and broad terraces overlooking the courtyard. Below: Exploded view and site plan.

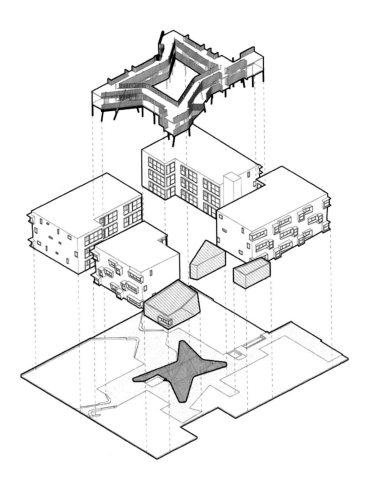

Above: West-facing windows, hooded to provide shade, have deep reveals.

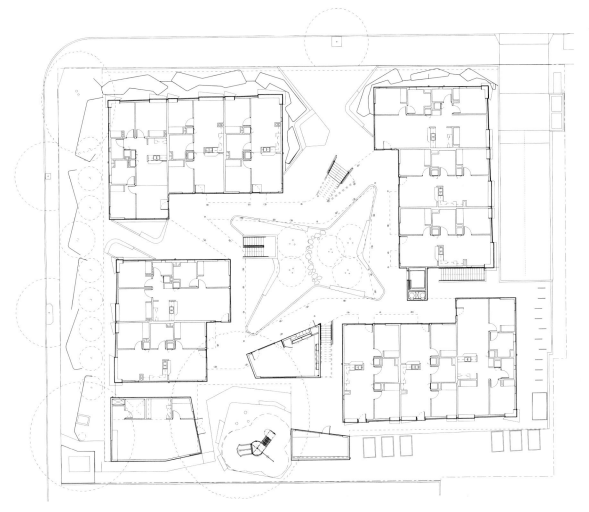

Based in Los Angeles, Lorcan O'Herlihy Architects was established in 1990. It has completed ten houses and twelve apartment buildings, as well as other varied projects, in Southern California and beyond.

LORCAN O'HERLIHY

REACHING OUT

Formosa, a condo block in West Hollywood, has an outer skin of red-painted metal and overlooks a pocket park.

Habitat 835 was sunk down a story and set back from the street to reduce its impact on the garden of R.M. Schindler's house-studio in West Hollywood.

"In thirty years, 75 percent of the world's population will be living in cities, so it's important to create housing that will exploit the full potential of urban life. Enlightened design elevates the soul and enriches the community. It's the subtle moves: filtering-in light, using tactile materials, making places that are nice to live in and foster optimism. That is the prime driver for all our buildings, and the people who live in them have a favorable response. Architecture should be from the inside out as well as the outside in. We are doing a project for the homeless in South Central Los Angeles, a very distressed area, and the quality is no different from the other buildings we've done. Architecture is for everybody.

"We try to combine affordability and creative solutions. You have to embrace the idea of repetition, and be inventive in the materials you use, staying on budget and schedule. Then you can free yourself to engage the sidewalk and the city, rather than push a dumb box to the building line. There should be an opportunity to cut into the block to pull in light and employ passive design strategies. A very simple move in one of our projects was to enclose a staircase with glass to create an interior light well from a 130 sq ft [12 sq m] space that couldn't be built on. It exploded with light; the quality of the space spoke volumes We can add architectural value without increasing the cost.

"When we design something that may prove difficult for the contractor, we do mock-ups and get vendors to commit to an assembled price. Then we use our powers of persuasion.

"Developers want the maximum return on their investment, so we've tried to persuade them that the more you bring in light, outdoor spaces, and the Southern California lifestyle, the greater the appeal to renters or buyers. There is a growing awareness that design sells. Some developers are

willing to take a risk and trust an architect to design a project well, within a reasonable budget. Every project is unique and my clients don't come with a formula. The target audience is getting younger and has different preferences. Studios and one-bedroom units are becoming more common.

"Apartments should reach out to the community. When we designed Habitat 835, adjoining [Austrian-born American architect] R.M. Schindler's classic house-studio, we pushed the building back 15 ft [4.5 m] and installed public benches in a landscaped forecourt. On a site a few blocks away, we set the Formosa back from a pocket park. West Hollywood is a very progressive city; it would be a challenge to do that in LA because the city would be responsible for maintaining the park. Once you break that public/private boundary you make a statement: the apartments become part of the neighborhood, rather than segregating themselves from the street.

"There has to be a balance of communality and privacy. At Habitat 835 there are three decks in front, and residents respect others' privacy—they see it as a community of friends. We doubled the conventional width of the access walkways so that people could bring out tables and chairs. The younger generation embrace that lifestyle. They thrive on cities, walking the streets, the convenience of having everything close to hand, rather than retreating from the bustle and driving to a suburb in search of quietude.

"We are working on mixed-use projects in New York and Detroit that incorporate apartments, as well as landscaping and open spaces, to have the best of both worlds. For a 135-unit project in Silver Lake [a community on the edge of downtown LA], we proposed that open spaces be dispersed, creating small social hubs for each of ten apartments rather than a single courtyard. When you work on a larger scale you don't have to have an overwhelming mass."

BUILDING BLOCKS

Most people would prefer to live in a house of their choosing or in a compact apartment building where they knew all their neighbors. That is becoming an unattainable ideal in big cities, where the demand for housing far exceeds the supply, and the cost of land drives ever larger developments. An extreme case is New York, where as many as half a million people live in huge public apartment blocks, and a million more in subsidized housing, often on an equally large scale. The best of these mega-blocks are thoughtfully planned and well maintained, by or for their residents, but few have much character. Tenants are grateful to have an affordable roof over their heads, but they deserve better.

Tight budgets may put a squeeze on creativity, but some architects have turned constraints to their advantage, creating buildings that enrich the townscape and enhance the experience of apartment living. These exceptional projects are scaled to their surroundings, helping to weave the urban fabric a little tighter and give it added richness. And they achieve this at every price level, from low income to affluent. The first modernists believed that everyone should enjoy a well-designed environment, and both the *Siedlungen* of 1920s Berlin and the best postwar estates in Britain proved that could be done on a large scale and at a reasonable cost. There is an urgent need to combine quality with quantity, and to balance profitability with social responsibility.

In Copenhagen, 8 House anchors the new quarter of Ørestad, and provides varied accommodation for as many as 1,500 people in a greatly enlarged version of the traditional courtyard block. It is a good demonstration of how Bjarke Ingels Group rethinks familiar forms. The Interlace in Singapore is even more ambitious, stacking horizontal bars in a hexagonal complex to stay within a mandatory height limit and exploiting a wooded site to best advantage.

In Amsterdam, NL Architects has created De Kameleon, a model block of apartments that opens onto a landscaped courtyard, and is rehabilitating 1960s blocks that were poorly maintained but are still structurally sound. On Chicago's South Side, Studio Gang's City Hyde Park offers a similar example of urban revitalization. A slab of market-rate apartments rises from the garden atop a retail podium, and the façades to north and south are designed to maximize light and views.

In Milan, Zaha Hadid's upscale apartments create a new enclave within the bounds of the city, and their free-flowing shapes express its tradition of creativity. On a much smaller scale, LOH Architects has shoehorned a block of apartments onto a tilted wedge of land in west Los Angeles, stepping them down to provide residents with three roof terraces. The block was inspired by a terraced courtyard complex that Richard Neutra placed on a steep hillside across the street eighty years previously, when the master-planned neighborhood was still undeveloped. In this belated tribute to a landmark, Lorcan O'Herlihy has respected the intimate character of Westwood Village and created a future classic.

CITYLIFE: DYNAMIC FLOW

Via Senofonte 2–4, Milan

Zaha Hadid Architects
2004–14

Milan is the most cosmopolitan of Italian cities—a hub of design and fashion, trade fairs and adventurous architecture. Its historic monuments, from Sant'Ambrogio to La Scala, are swallowed up in the expanse of later building, and the façade of the Gothic cathedral is a 19th-century pastiche. The Torre Velasca abstracts a medieval keep; the Pirelli Tower is as slim and elegant as a runway model. CityLife is an expression of that eclecticism and passion for *la bella figura*. It comprises Zaha Hadid's cluster of seven upscale apartment blocks, a trio of office towers by Hadid, Arata Isozaki, and Daniel Libeskind, plus a park. These architects, allied to a consortium of developers, won the bid to master-plan the former trade-fair grounds, a 0.4 sq mile (1 sq km) site, in 2006.

Hadid's apartments loop around a landscaped courtyard for residents, and this is sliced through by a public right of way that links park and street. As project architect Maurizio Meossi explains, "Our design evolved from the schematic competition-winning proposal, as we adjusted the boundaries of the plot, fleshed out ideas, and negotiated with the developers' marketing team. We played with the orientation and façades to maximize transparency for the outer face, to pull light and views into the living areas, and to achieve a feeling of intimacy in the inner courtyard."

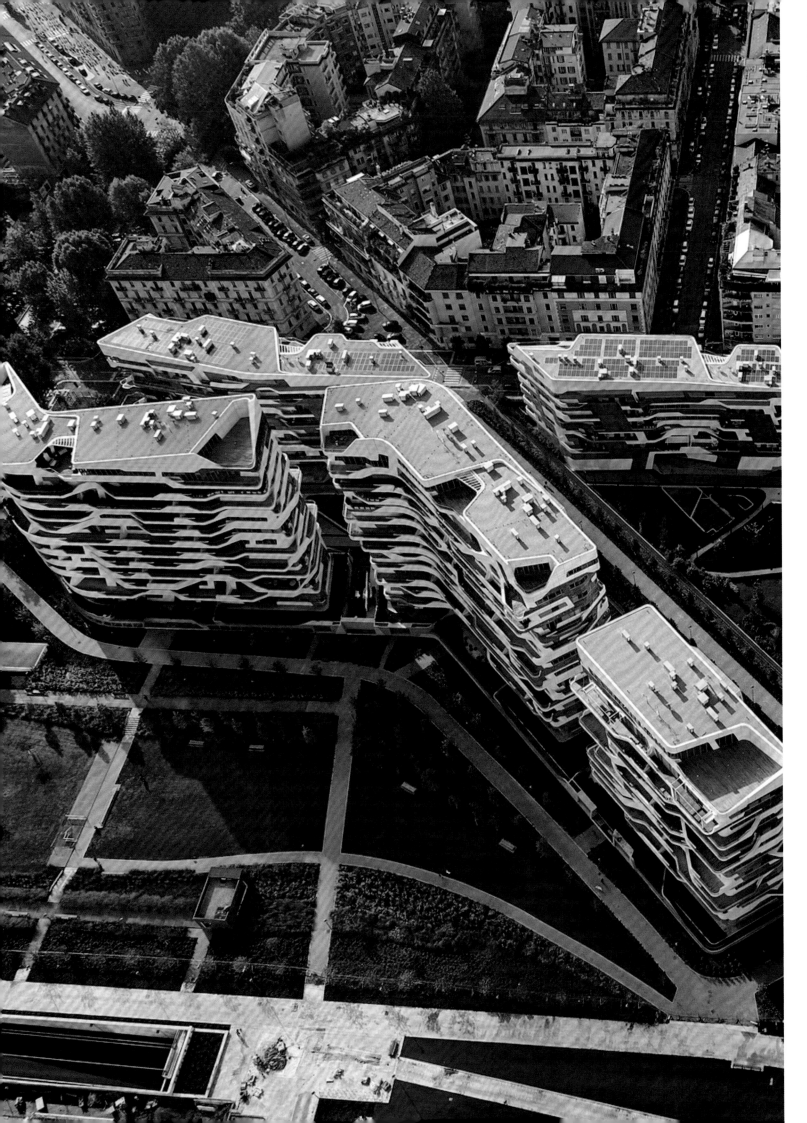

The residential part of the vast CityLife development is a complex of seven upscale apartment blocks on the former site of the Fiera Milano. Outer façades are clad in white-enameled panels, the inner face in untreated cedar.

Located on the south edge of the site, the apartment blocks range in height from five stories, where they play off existing buildings, to thirteen stories at the prow. This is oriented toward the office towers, whose verticality complements the emphatic horizontality of the apartments, with their curvilinear balconies and terraces. It is a reinterpretation of the stacked decks of ocean liners that inspired the pioneers of modernism, the prow conjuring up the image of a ship thrusting forward. The outer walls are clad in white-enameled aluminum panels, while the inner face is clad in untreated cedar that will weather to a silvery gray. The roofs are designed to be a fifth façade when viewed from the towers.

Although the blocks are enclosed in a boundary wall, they have a strong visual and physical connection to their surroundings. A network of underground parking keeps the surface streets traffic-free, and the buildings achieve a high level of sustainability. The new Tre Torri subway station is located in the podium of Hadid's tower, along with shops and an art gallery, and the park provides a welcome amenity in this densely built-up city. There are 230 apartments, ranging in size from 700 to 3,770 sq ft (65 to 350 sq m), and the duplex penthouses were the first to be sold. One potential buyer was frustrated that he could not have one that was 21,500 sq ft (2,000 sq m). Meossi and his team wanted to add a pool and roof gardens, but those amenities were eliminated, leaving only a meeting room and fitness center as shared spaces. That may encourage residents to support local businesses.

Hadid designed the double-height reception areas, which are bathed in light from floor-to-ceiling openings and display the sensuous flow of line that characterizes the firm's best work. She was not commissioned to design the apartment interiors, but she did shape the spaces, which mirror the sinuous geometry of the exterior. That should inspire residents and their interior designers to express themselves freely, playing off the architect's work. And it is probably just as well that she stopped there: too much of a good thing can be wonderful, as Mae West quipped, but there comes a point where one tires of a singular vision. A decade ago, Hadid designed a floor of the Puerta America Hotel in Madrid, creating an immersive environment of swooping lines. It offered adventurous guests a seamless transition from corridor to living area to a tub that swallowed up the unwary bather. An exhilarating experience for a short stay, but a little too assertive over the long haul. It was a reminder of Frank Lloyd Wright's insistence on designing every feature of a house, from roofs to foot stools, and even specifying what art his clients should hang on their walls.

Since then, Zaha Hadid Architects has worked on a much larger stage, designing a block of live–work apartments for Soho in Beijing, and the d'Leedon in Singapore, a mega-development of seven towers containing 1,715 units.

Section of the residential complex (below), which rises from five to fifteen stories, and a sample floor plan (opposite, top). Hadid designed the reception area (below, bottom); apartments were left to residents (opposite, bottom).

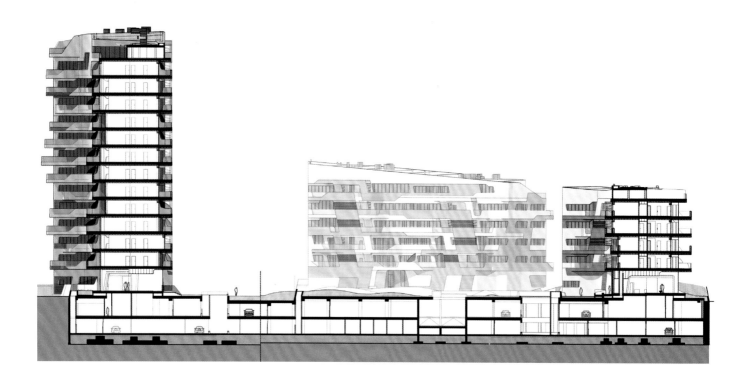

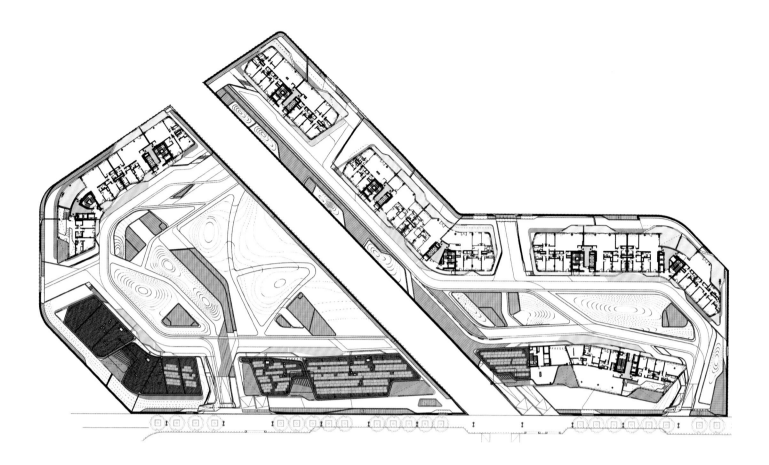

DE KAMELEON: NEIGHBORHOOD CATALYST

**Karspeldreef 1163–1465,
Bijlmer, Amsterdam**

**NL Architects
2006–13**

The city of Amsterdam has been steadily expanding beyond its historic core for the past century, acquiring additional layers like the rings of a tree. The process has accelerated in recent decades, driven by high land values, a growing number of immigrants, and, as in so many European port cities, the opportunity to redevelop former docklands. Master-planned by city authorities and consistently progressive in design, most of these new quarters have enriched the city. One visionary scheme that fell short was the Bijlmer, a neighborhood of concrete slab blocks erected in the 1960s and quickly inhabited by immigrants from former Dutch colonies. Located to the south of the center and initially isolated by a lack of public transportation, it was soon perceived as a ghetto and a dangerous place to go.

To remedy the ills, planners decreed that most of the ten-story blocks should be torn down and replaced by low-rise housing that would also occupy the green spaces in between. Only one horseshoe complex of six linked blocks, now dubbed the Bijlmer Museum, was saved, thanks to a group of young developers who upgraded the exterior galleries, elevators, and infrastructure, while allowing about 500 residents to buy their apartments at a very low price and pay for the interior improvements themselves. Kamiel Klasse, a partner in NL Architects, became deeply involved in this surgical intervention, supervising the rehabilitation of the old blocks, as well as winning a competition to replace a decrepit garage-supermarket with a new structure.

De Kameleon is a mixed-use building measuring 160 × 590 ft (50 × 180 m) on plan, located on the main commercial street of Bijlmer, adjoining an elevated subway station. A complex of apartments rising from a podium of retail and parking, it is intended as a catalyst—a gesture of confidence by the city that has attracted a diversity of residents, including people who wanted a better place to live without leaving the neighborhood. Klasse has drawn on his love of the Amsterdam School to create a 230-unit block that is humanized by its impeccably crafted yellow brick piers and interior garden atop the podium. The piers are in three widths, spaced at 25 ft (8 m) intervals to create a rhythm that is amplified by the zig-zag projecting bays.

"When I was studying in the eighties, there was no way you could use brick," recalls Klasse. "To me, it's a wonderful experience to cycle from home to work through the beautiful neighborhoods of the 1910s—playful, poetic, stunningly detailed buildings." His great achievement was to revive this tradition on a much larger scale and save money through repetition to cover the higher cost of the brickwork.

Klasse has mixed feelings about apartment living: "I grew up in a spacious farmhouse with a big garden. We now live on the eighth floor and overlook the city on both sides. My kids love seeing the sun rise and the fog rolling in, but when they were small they had to play on a gallery, not the street." To make high-rise living more attractive, the larger apartments are concentrated in the low wings, accessed from galleries that are divided into short lengths to promote neighborliness. They face outward and into the garden, which has twelve large trees and a stream running through it. One of the wings blocks noise from the busy street; the other is broken open to accommodate play and barbecue areas. At the eastern end of the complex, a ten-story slab rises from the low block, serving as a "billboard" for De Kameleon. A large opening at the base frames the subway station platforms, providing a visual link to the world beyond. Private balconies and varied fenestration on the side elevations break up the mass of the building and give residents a sense of openness.

Every aspect of the building has been carefully thought through. The former supermarket was a hermetic container; the new one comprises many smaller units, each with its own street frontage. An interior circulation route makes a double loop, and escalators link it to an upper floor, with retail at one end and a food court and fitness center at the other. Sandwiched between are two levels of parking for customers and residents, with open sides for natural ventilation.

A slab block and two wings atop two levels of retail overlook a landscaped courtyard (overleaf, top). Balconies are angled to animate the façades and open up views.

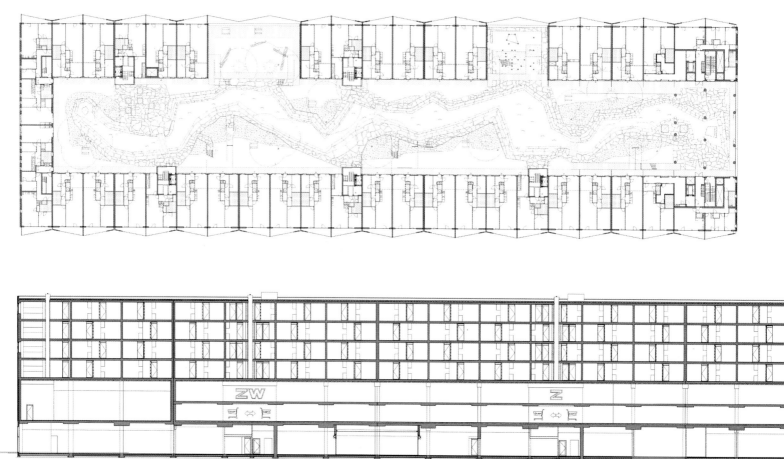

Apartments extend the full width of the wings, providing cross-ventilation and abundant natural light. Opposite and below: Sample floor plan and section.

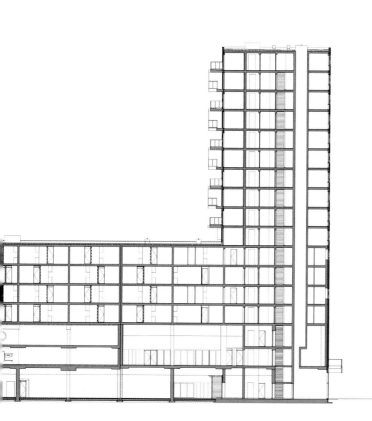

CITY HYDE PARK: LIVABLE LANDMARK

5105 S. Harper Avenue, Chicago

Studio Gang
2005–16

Restrained invention has been the hallmark of Chicago since the city was rebuilt following the devastating fire of 1871. Landmark buildings by Louis Sullivan, Frank Lloyd Wright, and Mies van der Rohe are standouts in a city master-planned by architect Daniel Burnham to be a model of urbanity. Mies's towers on Lake Shore Drive (1949–51) and Bertrand Goldberg's Marina City (early 1960s) raised the bar on apartment living, as did the more recent Contemporaine of Perkins + Will (page 23). Studio Gang has built on these solid foundations, first with the Aqua Tower (2010) and, most recently, City Hyde Park, a block of 180 apartments near the University of Chicago campus on the South Side.

Principal Jeanne Gang wanted to recreate two-thirds of a city block that was formerly occupied by a strip mall and surface parking, to achieve a lively mix of activities and increased urban density. Underground parking allowed the city to broaden the sidewalks on three sides. Her chief goal was to provide affordable apartments in a multicultural neighborhood—formerly home to Barack Obama—where demand far exceeds supply. She had earlier converted several historic buildings for Eli Ungar of Antheas Capital, and his support was indispensable in securing approval for a bold design and bringing it to completion after the financial crisis nearly derailed the project.

A twelve-story slab block rises from the northern side of a two-story podium of retail and offices with a landscaped roof. The concept is similar to De Kameleon (page 77), as are the angled bays, and there is even an elevated metro station to one side, but the structural system has its own unique character. Frigid winters and torrid summers challenge Chicago architects to create buildings that are well protected and adapt to every season. The north side of City Hyde Park has wide bays to pull in light and expansive views of the Chicago skyline. The south-facing apartments open onto cantilevered balconies that are framed by slender concrete planes in a lively interplay of vertical and horizontal elements.

When the project was put on hold in 2009, Studio Gang was asked to make deep cuts—the kind of value engineering that typically compromises the architectural quality of a building. The architects and their engineer responded by refining their design, paring a couple of centimeters from every part of the structure and turning constraints to advantage. As a result, the building has a taut elegance that cost less and delivers more. To conceal structural columns that would have blocked views, and to make the apartment interiors feel more spacious, the architects devised a system they call "wallumns"—a combination of walls and columns. To the north, these are integrated within the sheer façade; to the south, they form an exostructure that provides shade and privacy while encouraging residents to step outside and socialize with their neighbors. The slender planes are lightly tied back to the floor slabs with a thermal barrier between. Fritted glass balustrades add another layer to the composition and reduce bird strikes.

In the original design, the upper level of the retail–office podium was clad in copper. As an economy, the architects substituted a tile mosaic with colors inspired by the seasonal changes of the trees. Residents enjoy 5,000 sq ft (465 sq m) of shared spaces at the base of the slab, and these open onto a terrace and a children's play area. Railing off the roof garden allowed the whole expanse to be densely planted, eliminating the stairs and reinforcement that would have been required for public access. It becomes a fifth façade when viewed from above. Apartments range in size from 580 sq ft (54 sq m) studios to 1,500 sq ft (139 sq m) three-bedroom units, with a variety of layouts. Sustainable features include storm-water capture, high-performance glass, and added insulation.

"I wanted to work from the inside out and we were able to shape the interiors and control the finishes," says Gang. "People were so eager to live here that rents are the highest in Hyde Park, though 20 percent of the apartments are reserved for low-income tenants." That duplicates the success of Aqua, where resale prices match those of the Trump Tower, a gaudy excrescence on a prominent downtown site, where the construction budget was three times higher. Good design always adds value.

On the south façade of the slab block (below), concrete walls and columns are combined to create generous balconies. To the north (opposite), angled bay windows frame sweeping views of downtown Chicago.

This page: Beneath the south-facing balconies is a terrace extending out from the residents' communal facilities and overlooking the landscaped roof of a two-story retail podium. Opposite: Sample floor plan, roof plan, and section.

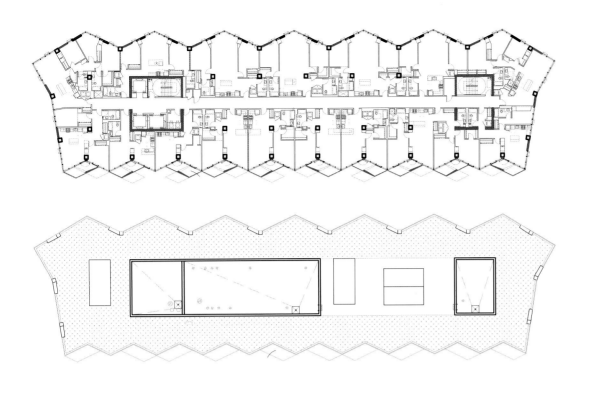

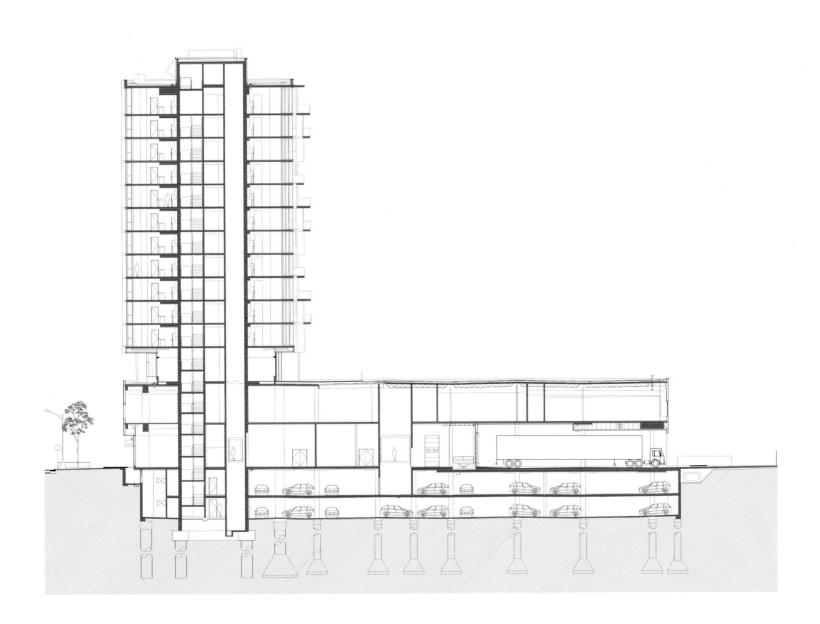

STUDIO 11024: TERRACED WEDGE

11024 Strathmore Drive, Los Angeles

LOH Architects 2012–15

Residential neighborhoods all over Southern California are losing their character as owners and developers relentlessly exploit escalating land values. North Westwood Village, which was master-planned in the 1920s as a small-scale community of rental properties, has been particularly hard-hit. The municipal code mandates harmonious development, but that requirement was generally ignored from the 1960s onward, as hills were carved away and big-box student rooming houses overwhelmed neighboring properties and narrow, winding streets. Development was largely driven by the explosive

growth of UCLA (University of California, Los Angeles) and its behemoth medical center.

After half a century of abuse, the North Village has finally acquired an architectural gem, Studio 11024, located across the street from Richard Neutra's landmark Strathmore Apartments. It required legal action by a neighborhood association to compel the developer to abandon the eyesore he had proposed and commission a new design from Lorcan O'Herlihy Architects. The challenge was to fit thirty-one units totaling 37,000 sq ft (3,440 sq m) onto a narrow, tilted wedge of land, stepping down from six to two stories in deference to Neutra's garden court of eight units terraced up a steep slope. It was a reprise of LOHA's Habitat 835 (page 67) on Kings Road in West Hollywood, where the site was excavated a story so that the new block would not overshadow the garden of R.M. Schindler's classic studio-house.

"On Strathmore we asked, 'What if we cut into the box and landscaped the different roof levels, allowing residents to engage the outdoors?'" says O'Herlihy. That is a concept as old as the Native American pueblos of the Southwest and the roof gardens of North Africa and the Middle East, but one that has been largely forgotten in the rush to fill every square meter of rentable space. The city mandates a 50 ft (15 m)

wide view corridor through a block that is more than 150 ft (45 m) long. LOHA reinterpreted this rule to create a linear divide, which accommodates outdoor walkways and stairs linking three roof gardens, and reduces the need for double-loaded corridors. Half the apartments have opening windows on two sides for abundant natural light and cross-ventilation. There are two levels of underground parking, as well as a lower-level gym and business center.

Most LA houses and apartment buildings are faced in stucco, all too often in beige tones. Although the budget was tight, LOHA discovered that the structure could be clad in ribbed, white-enameled aluminum panels for little more than a standard stucco finish ($160 vs $130 per sq m [11 sq ft]). The panels are deployed on the two street façades in tiers of differently sized ribs. Those variations serve to break up the mass of the conjoined blocks. Lateral cuts function as backdrops to the roof terraces and are clad with Hardie board, layered in six tones of yellowish green that become lighter as they ascend. The white echoes the Neutra and several neighboring blocks, and as a mix of all the colors it responds to changes of light. Handrails and metal staircases pick up on the green walls, which introduce a vibrant new element into the townscape. Perforated white metal panels screen the

staircases, teak benches divide up the terraces, and the sharp edges are softened by landscape designer Mia Lehrer's generous plantings.

Nearly all LA apartment blocks are as repetitive as a motel, but LOHA insists on diversified interiors, ranging from studios to lofts. O'Herlihy—like Michael Maltzan, Kevin Daly, and other contemporaries—understands that a younger generation wants to break free of the conventional layouts imposed on their parents. On Strathmore, the two- and three-bedroom apartments were configured by the developer's interior consultant, but the plans are varied, and there are three duplex apartments on the fifth floor.

Studio 11024 is a deceptively complex building with well-varied fenestration that responds organically to the shifts of elevation and orientation. From the street, it reads as a stepped wedge rather than parallel blocks, but it is a form that is constantly altering as you move around it, as well as in response to changes of light and the play of sun and shadow through the trees. It achieves a high level of sustainability and raises the bar for Westwood Village, showing how architecture adds value for owners, tenants, and neighbors. Ideally, it will attract a lively mix of residents, and encourage other developers to aim higher by hiring talented architects.

Open stairs link each level of decks and walkways in this stepped-back wedge of apartments. Exterior façades are clad in white-enameled panels, ribbed to catch the light, and inner walls are painted green or clad in multi-toned Hardie board.

Opposite: Three duplex apartments open off the fifth-level walkway and overlook the expansive wooden decks. The constraints of the tapered site are turned to advantage and the block achieves a high level of sustainability.
Below: Section and sample floor plan.

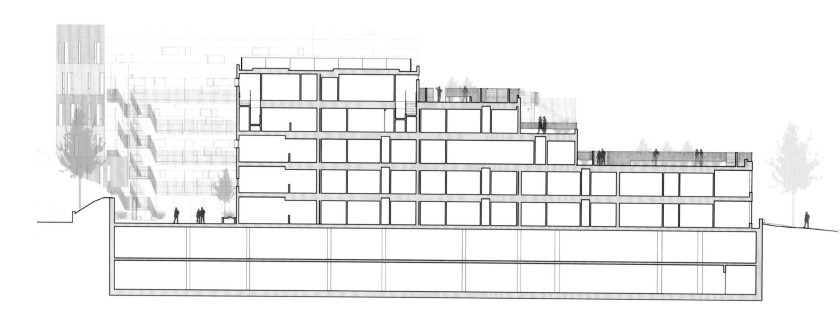

A complex of varied living units rises from lower levels of retail and offices, with broad ramps ascending around the courtyards to the top floors.

8 HOUSE: GENTLE GIANT

Richard Mortensens Vej 61, Copenhagen

Bjarke Ingels Group (BIG) 2007–11

Western port cities are transforming their waterfronts, as dock facilities are relocated to serve container ships. In Copenhagen, this has freed up the island of Amager between the old city and the airport for the linear planned community of Ørestad. Anchoring its south end is 8 House, a complex of housing, offices, and shops that takes its name from the way it is wrapped in a figure-eight around twin courtyards. The competition-winning design by the Bjarke Ingels Group (BIG) boosted the firm's reputation worldwide, and it has greatly expanded the scope and scale of its activities over the past five years, from both its base in Copenhagen and a flourishing New York office. Ingels made his reputation as the *enfant terrible* of Danish architecture, rejecting what he calls "the Arne Jacobsen legacy of simple boxes with perfectly crafted door knobs." Like those of his former boss, Rem Koolhaas, Ingels's designs evolve organically as exercises in problem-solving, rather than the expression of an aesthetic.

8 House is the third BIG residential project for Per Hoepfner, a savvy developer who calculated what first-time buyers could afford to pay and looked for ways to build cheaply and well within that budget. "He knows a lot about building technology and he's not afraid to experiment and do things differently, just as long as it works," says Ingels. 8 House is the largest and most accessible of the three, providing its thousand residents and many day workers with a range of amenities. It is a bold rethinking of the perimeter block that is a familiar feature of Copenhagen.

"When you are constructing a city from scratch, it's important to have spaces and places for reference and for public life," says Ingels. "In building on such a large scale, we wanted to design 8 House not as a beautiful object, but to stimulate social intercourse." To achieve this, the architects have created an urban layer cake in which each element has its appropriate place. Retail occupies the bottom level with exposure to shoppers and delivery trucks. The entire ground level is accessible to the public. Neighbors can shop, work, and play there, and bring their children to the kindergarten that spills out into the north courtyard, with a playground that all can use after school hours. The courtyards are landscaped, with grassy knolls and birch trees to the north, varied trees and lawns to the south. The master plan mandates that cars be parked off-site. Residents and visitors are encouraged to use the metro, which runs twenty-four hours a day and will eventually be extended to put 80 percent of Copenhagen's population within 650 yards (600 m) of a station.

Offices need a little more quiet and privacy, so they are located on the next level up from the retail; residents crave abundant light and views, so they occupy the upper stories. Everything is linked by corner staircases, elevators, and ramps that converge on the central crossing and then ascend to the upper levels to provide pedestrian streets for wheelchairs, baby strollers, and bicycles. Ingels describes this gently inclined path as an infinity loop, and it may have been inspired by his experience in helping design the ramp that runs up through OMA's Seattle Library. Residents have formed an association to manage the communal facilities, which include meeting and party rooms, a day-care facility, and guest accommodations in the central crossing, plus a roof terrace.

To keep construction costs to about 1,300 euros per sq m (11 sq ft), 8 House was assembled from prefabricated concrete wall and floor panels like a giant Lego set, with modular infill elements of wood, glass, and brushed aluminum. Conventional materials are employed in interesting ways. Different finishes and tones are used on the aluminum fascias, and black and white tiles create a pixelated version of the swirling pavement designs of Roberto Burle Marx on the Rio de Janeiro waterfront. Within the courtyards the scale is humane, and BIG has cleverly exploited the mix of 475 dwelling units to introduce a variety of façades. Townhouses open onto walled front yards with small trees in planters. The apartments of various sizes and configurations are stacked above, with penthouses at the top. The bulk of 8 House, which rises to eleven stories at its highest point and looms over vacant lots, will be largely concealed when those sites are built out over the next decade. Only the southwest corner, which is sharply cut away to frame views over Amager Common and pull in sunlight, will be seen from afar.

Landscaped courtyards are open to the public and provide safe play areas for children. The southwest end is cut away to open up views of open fields and pull in sunlight.

Below (top and center): Section and sample floor plan. Below (bottom) and opposite: Staircases and ramps promote social interchange among the residents and foster a strong sense of place.

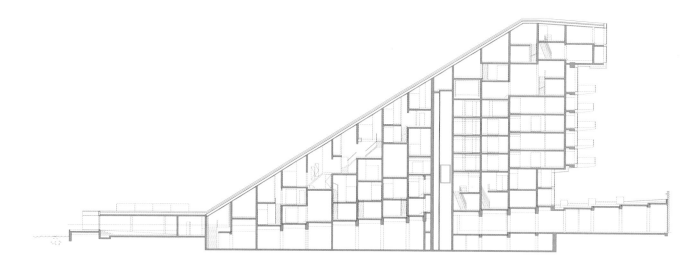

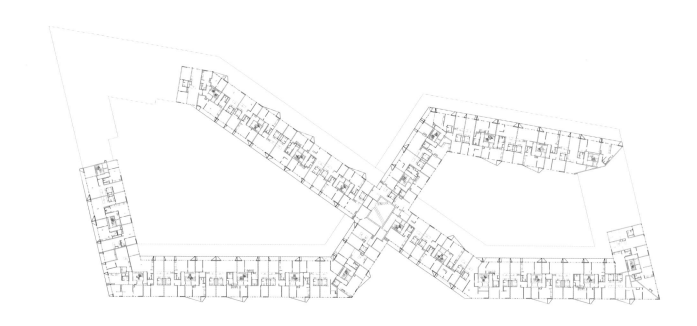

Six-story bars of apartments are stacked at the corners to enclose hexagonal courtyards that provide a variety of spaces in which to play and relax.

THE INTERLACE: ENGAGING MEGASTRUCTURE

200 Depot Road, Singapore

OMA/Ole Scheeren
2007–13

The Interlace is located outside the commercial center of Singapore in a green belt that has a twenty-four-story height limit. As architect Ole Scheeren explains, "The developer wanted 1,040 units on the 8 hectare [20 acre] site and the conventional way would have been a cluster of twelve towers—a miniature high-rise city with too little space between and no privacy for residents. The solution was to turn vertical into horizontal; stacked bars that would generate a diversity of urban spaces. We wanted togetherness, not isolation; a return to when Singapore was a village of little buildings, tightly knit together."

Ten years ago, Ole Scheeren was a partner in OMA's Beijing office, supervising construction of the CCTV Tower, when he decided to explore the idea of designing affordable housing for Asian developers. He was dismayed by the way that planning regulations and economic forces produced formulaic responses—a forest of vertical extrusions. CapitaLand invited him to design one of the largest residential projects ever undertaken in Singapore, and he seized the chance to put his ideas into practice. Convincing the client to approve a radical alternative was a struggle, but the profitability and critical success of the Interlace (which won the WAF Building of the Year award) launched his practice, Büro Ole Scheeren.

The Interlace comprises thirty-one six-story bars, identical in size, which are stacked two to four blocks high. They overlap at the ends and are supported on mega-columns

that surround service cores. The columns function like the legs of a table, supporting 6 ft (2 m) thick, post-tensioned concrete slabs. The first bar was a challenge to build, but after that construction was fast and efficient, coming in on budget and more than two months ahead of schedule. To hold down costs and make the apartments affordable, Scheeren economized on materials. Uniform concrete façades have a resilient paint finish. Much time was spent studying the impact of the sun, optimizing the glazing for solar and acoustic insulation, to save money and energy. Parking and traffic circulation are concealed in a subterranean level that has openings to the sky to provide natural ventilation.

In photographs, the Interlace seems to embody a utopian vision—reminiscent of the Russian Constructivists and the Japanese Metabolists, whose designs were mostly confined to paper. But those were schematic, theory-driven schemes. Scheeren's priorities are community and quality of life, within the varied units—which range from 800 to 6,300 sq ft (75 to 585 sq m)—and the abundant open spaces. There are eight hexagonal courtyards, and the void created by the missing thirty-second bar is occupied by an Olympic-size swimming pool. The widely spaced bars allow light and fresh air to penetrate every part of the complex. Water bodies have been located within wind corridors to promote evaporative cooling and the creation of microclimates. Green roofs and lush plantings augment the tropical forest that surrounds the complex. There is 10 percent more greenery on site than before the building went up.

"Diversity balances the rigor of the structure," says Scheeren. "You can choose where you want to live— socializing in a well-trafficked area, or hiding away in a less-frequented space, and there are many different views. All the units have balconies or terraces. Each courtyard has its own character, and that gives every resident a sense of identity. And the Interlace is 90 percent occupied [about sixty of the residents are employees of CapitaLand], unlike many upscale towers that have become ghost towns because apartments are bought for speculation and sit empty."

For Scheeren, the Interlace is a prototype for affordable living, and its commercial success should encourage developers—in both Asia and the West—to be more adventurous. An architect has no incentive to create good living environments in luxury towers that are merely trading counters, but he or she has every reason to apply intelligence to something meaningful. Scheeren's own experience of living in eight countries and engaging different cultures has taught him what works and what concepts should be explored. And he has honed his ideas as a visiting professor, teaching a course in Hong Kong called "Core Values." Nearing completion in Vancouver is a tower that occupies a small footprint but achieves a feeling of spatial drama by shifting apartments off the vertical axis.

Green roofs, lush plantings, and water features augment the tropical forest that surrounds the property and enhance its environmental quality. A pool (opposite, bottom) takes the place of one bar of apartments at the base of the complex.

The horizontality and generous open spaces of the Interlace create
a much richer environment than a conventional cluster of tower blocks.

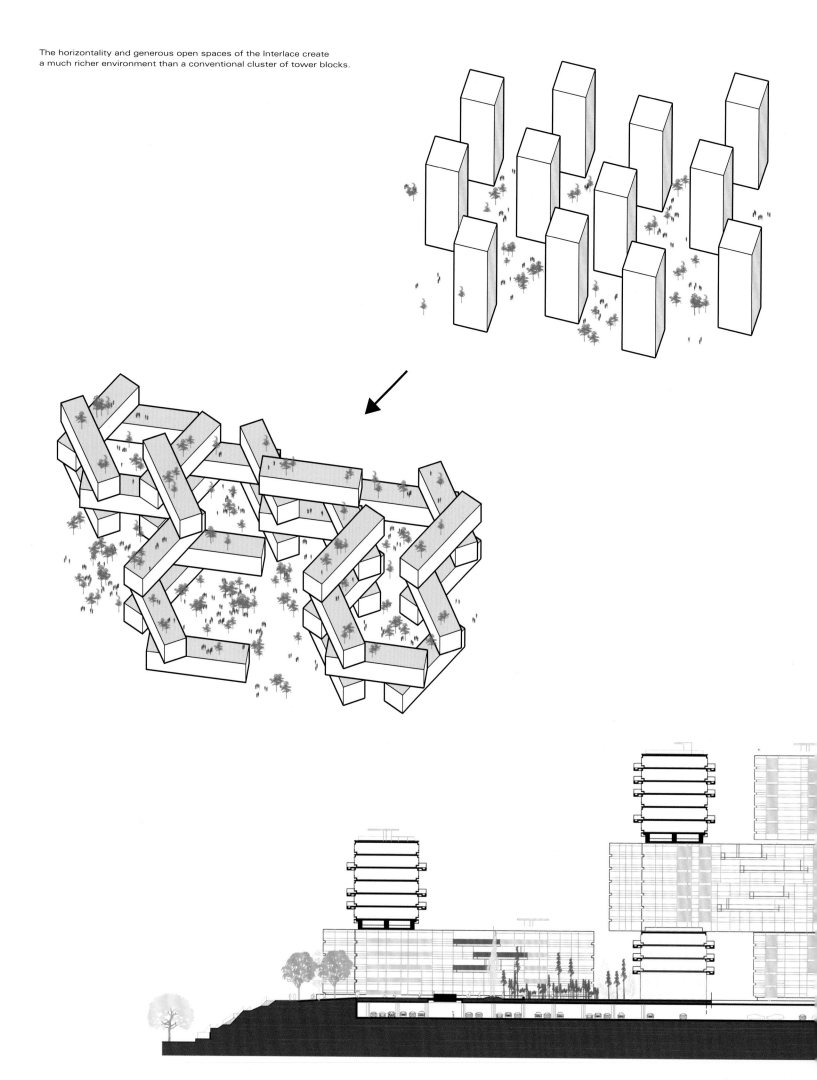

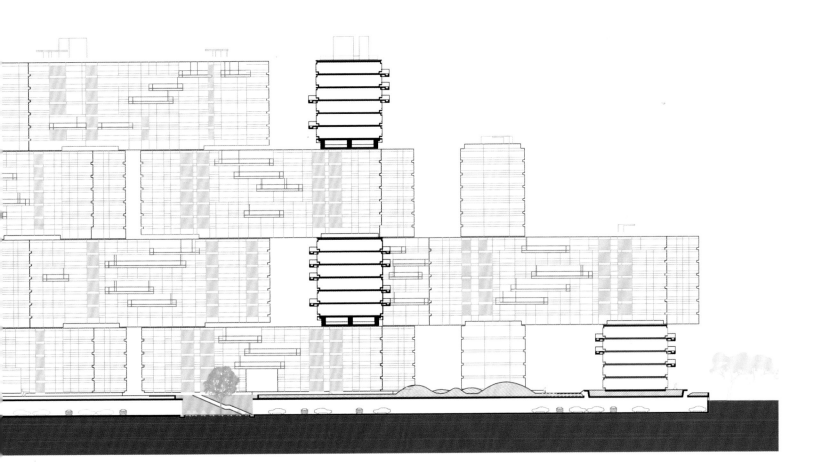

BIG, the Bjarke Ingels Group, was established in Copenhagen in 2005, and opened its New York office in 2011. Among its many innovative projects, a complex of vacation apartments in Hualien, Taiwan, is conceived as an extension of the landscape, while new apartments atop a concrete warehouse in Basel are rotated to open up views and pull in more light.

BJARKE INGELS

EXPLOITING IRREGULARITY

Mountain, a stepped apartment block in Copenhagen.

"All building regulations are rigid and all developers are profit-oriented. Those are the rules of the game. Multi-family housing is a challenge because the margins are very tight, and developers' fear of not being able to move their product reinforces the lowest common denominator. If you can find a client who is willing to think differently, then there is room to innovate. In each case we've chosen one experiment we want to realize and we do everything else as simply and rationally as possible. Every time an alternative succeeds it opens a whole avenue of possibilities for others to follow suit.

"In a hill town on the Mediterranean, like Amalfi, the different homes have grown together in a continuous mass and adapt to the natural topography. That provides a lot of quirkiness, charm, and irregularity. It's not about designing one perfect unit and repeating it five hundred times, but trying to optimize unique configurations in the best possible way. In 8 House [page 96] there are sloping roofs and living rooms that rise from 6 ft [2 m] in one corner to 18 ft [6 m] in the opposite corner. It's like living in a chalet in the middle of the city. Working simultaneously inside-out and outside-in provides you with units that have the lively character you find in old villages but rarely in new developments.

"I bought an apartment for myself that is a freak of the New York zoning regulations. A rooftop unit on a new seven-story block near the Manhattan Bridge. It's 100 ft [30 m] long, 18 ft [6 m] wide, and partly double-height. It receives light from all four sides, and opens onto a terrace that is more than 2,000 sq ft [186 sq m]. By Danish standards, New York has eight months of summer, so it's wonderful to have so much outdoor space.

"We realized a trilogy of apartment buildings in Copenhagen, and one triggered the next. At VM we were given a target price of around $900 per sq m [11 sq ft], and because the client was so concerned to do it cheaply he was willing to accept things that were out of the ordinary. The apartments are 50 ft [16 m] deep—much more than usual—and the living areas double-height, so that we could access three levels from one corridor, as in Le Corbusier's Unité d'Habitation. We saved money on circulation, and the rawness gave the apartments the quality of lofts, even though there are 150 different configurations—a three-dimensional puzzle.

"The next, Mountain, was conceived as units added to a neighborhood parking structure. We decided to make them unique, not by varied plans, but by providing as much outdoor as indoor space. That gave them the feeling of a house with a garden, plus a penthouse view. 8 House comprises 360 apartments and 150 townhouses in an entirely new neighborhood, and the goal was to create social interaction between the residents. By Danish standards, it is very dense, rising to eleven stories, so we lowered the southwest corner to pull in light and open up views.

"Our practice, like the city, is a work in progress. The Durst block on West 57th Street in New York [VIA 57 WEST] has some of the same ideas as 8 House, adapted to the context of Manhattan. It's four times as high, much denser, and surrounded by apartment towers and a busy highway. So the challenge was to create an oasis in the middle of the city. We wanted to create a sense of place for the residents, with their own little Central Park. The courtyard is communal, not public. At 8 House, a ramp climbs to the top; here, there are terraces recessed into the roofs, so residents can enjoy privacy and the opportunity to walk to the edge and chat to their neighbors. Durst will own the building, so they care about the long-term issues. They are interested in lasting attributes: energy efficiency, durability, and sustainability. And that makes them incredibly interesting to work with."

VIA 57 WEST in Manhattan, overlooking the Hudson River.

PROMOTING SOCIABILITY

The decline of suburbia and the renewed appreciation of inner cities have created new markets for apartment living. Singles, creatives, students, and seniors tend to have limited incomes and space requirements. Those with disabilities and the formerly homeless have special needs. All these groups crave a sense of community. That has challenged architects to explore novel combinations of public and private space—often finding inspiration in the idealism of the early modern movement.

Moisei Ginzburg's Narkomfin, an experimental housing complex of 1928 for government workers in Moscow, took the idea of communal living to its logical extreme. Now decrepit, it survives as a monument to the Soviet regime's failure to remold its citizens as cogs in a state-run machine. Collectivism has taken a voluntary turn in several German cities, especially Berlin, with the proliferation of *Baugruppen*, or building groups. Typically, a group of friends hold meetings to define their wishes and needs, then acquire a plot of land and commission an architect to build them a tightly budgeted block of apartments. As the product of consensus, these *Baugruppen* rarely stray far beyond the basics, but they offer an affordable alternative to commercial developments and a sense of shared purpose.

Exemplary architecture can create a sense of community at every scale. Fernando Barnuevo is a Spanish aficionado of modernism who divides his time between Madrid and New York. He bought and restored the compact house that Ulrich Franzen designed for himself in 1958 in Rye, New York, and moved in with his large family, inviting them to pretend they were sailing around the world on a small boat. No longer did the children retreat to their individual rooms to watch TV or play video games, but joined together to play in the garden or the living room.

This chapter offers six examples of how architects can foster a sense of community for very different groups of people. Tietgen, a hollow cylinder of student rooms in Copenhagen, is a model of communal living, offering residents a menu of choices, from single rooms and kitchen-eating areas for small groups of neighbors to a landscaped courtyard overlooked by balconies. On the other side of the world, in Seoul, Songpa comprises a dense cluster of micro-apartments with breakout areas on every level to bring residents together.

A group of architects in Melbourne developed the Commons as an affordable place where they and like-minded people could live comfortably, as well as socialize in a rooftop garden and a downstairs café. In San Diego, an architect who has specialized in housing the homeless developed a small urban site for himself, as a layering of parking, office, and two apartments, all opening onto a courtyard that hosts parties and neighborhood events.

The Star Apartments are located just off Skid Row in downtown Los Angeles, providing humane housing for the homeless atop a podium of service facilities, with community rooms, a garden, and a running track to act as a buffer between the street and prefabricated living units. In Paris, the Hérold social housing blocks open onto a richly landscaped garden, with ground-floor apartments reserved for those with disabilities.

TIETGEN STUDENT HALL: SOCIAL CONDENSER

Rued Langgaards Vej, Copenhagen

Lundgaard & Tranberg Arkitekter
2002–06

Most student dorms are generic and spartan, but Tietgen would generate a huge demand if it were put on the market. A hollow cylinder, comprising six stories of single rooms, rises from a ground floor of shared spaces and basement parking. It is located in Ørestad Nord near the new Copenhagen and IT university campuses, and it stands out sharply from its prosaic neighbors in this raw waterfront development. Ørestad is still a work in progress, and the master plan is disappointingly schematic, but there is a scatter of exemplary buildings, notably the three apartment blocks by BIG, whose

8 House (page 96) anchors the south end of Ørestad. Tietgen was designed by Lundgaard & Tranberg and built with a large donation from the Nordea Danmark Foundation as a model for "the dormitory of the future." Its form evokes another circular building type: the tulou of Fujian province in southern China. Those collective dwellings have a strong defensive character, with massive outer walls of rammed earth and a single, well-protected entry. In Shenzhen, Urbanus used the same model for workers' housing, but that, too, is impenetrable.

By contrast, Tietgen radiates transparency and openness, with a lively alternation of projecting bays and recessed balconies on the outer façade. Double-height communal rooms and kitchens are cantilevered from the inner face, like theater boxes overlooking a stage. The concrete frame construction is clad in tombac, a copper–zinc alloy that acquires a dark patina, and the shutters and joinery are oil-treated American oak. As the architects note, "The darker a building becomes, the more it gathers form, and the more the eyes—the windows—are apparent and thereby the building's pulsating life." The animation of the glass, metal, and wood façades, the constant movement, and the satisfying sense of enclosure make Tietgen an exemplary social condenser.

Five portals provide access to the upper levels and the grassy courtyard, which is encircled by a walkway and broad wooden bench. The ground floor includes a laundry, study and meeting rooms, bicycle storage, and an assembly hall. On each of the upper floors, sixty linear rooms radiate out from an inner corridor to the perimeter. Each group of twelve shares a kitchen–eating area with a balcony, and the continuity of the plan encourages every resident to socialize—in corridors, community areas, and, most of all, the courtyard.

There is a long tradition of thoughtful architecture and finely crafted buildings in Denmark, and Tietgen enriches that legacy. Boje Lundgaard died before the building was completed, but co-principal Lene Tranberg recalls the vision they brought to the competition. "We got the idea of a round building quite early in the process, but we were afraid that it was a little too radical for the jury [and] that we would not be respecting the zoning laws for the area." However, the client was looking for ideas rather than a fully-fledged scheme and wanted something exceptional.

In the year of intense collaboration that followed, the design evolved from a complex interweaving of apartment types to a repetitive cellular structure, in which every room is essentially similar. The driving idea was to get people out of their cells and into group activities. Each room is tapered, which makes it appear larger. Hand-finished plywood cabinetry occupies one side; on the other is a semicircular shower that projects out from the bathroom. Curtains in varied colors supplement the sliding wood shutters. Floors throughout the building are covered in wear-resistant magnesite; the ceilings are smooth concrete. The white-stained plywood on the inner face of the corridors has a subtle inkjet mural of Japanese leaves, created by designers Aggebo & Henriksen, who also created the bold graphics.

Tietgen is a model not only for student accommodation but also for affordable housing. Singles and seniors would relish the sociability and the strong sense of place. It would be easy to imagine a cluster of such circular blocks, varied in size and height, creating a new version of Le Corbusier's Ville Radieuse. Tietgen was an expensive project with exceptional finishes and detailing, made possible by the foundation grant. But it uses robust materials, and the plan could be further simplified to reduce the construction budget without sacrificing its unique qualities.

A hollow cylinder of student rooms rises from communal facilities
on the ground level. Each group of twelve rooms is accessed from
a staircase and shares a kitchen; balconies enable outdoor eating.

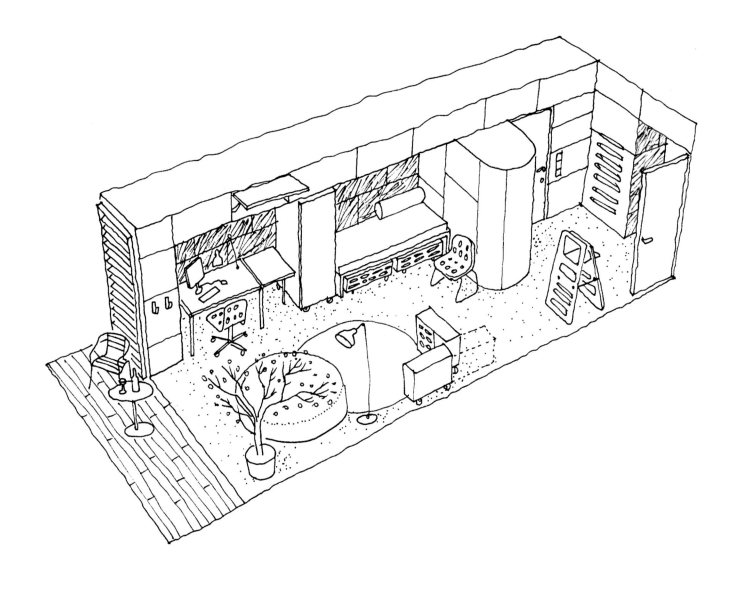

Single rooms are tapered segments of the circle, extending full width, and are fully furnished and equipped. The whole complex has been designed to promote social interaction. Opposite (top and bottom right): Section and sample floor plan.

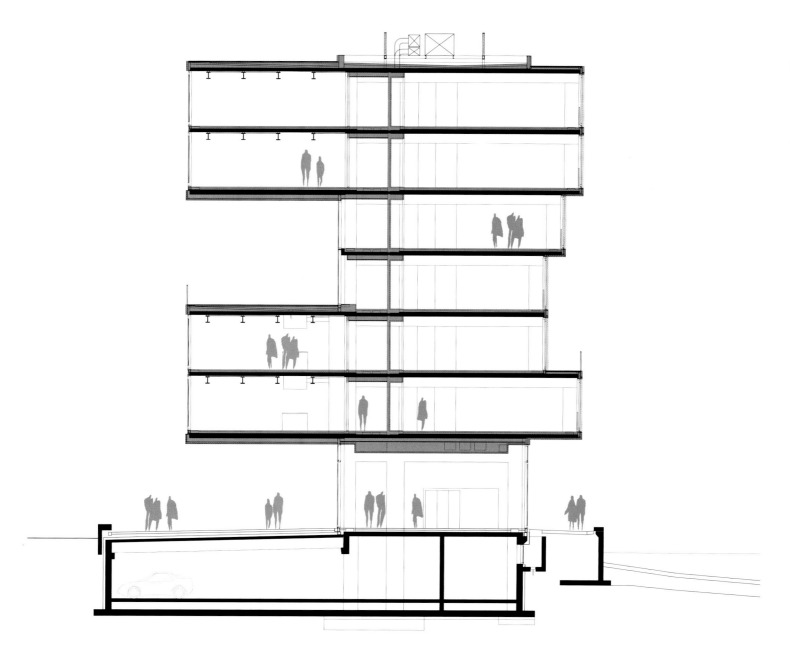

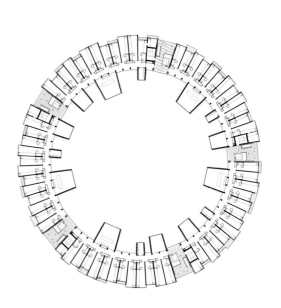

THE COMMONS: BOHEMIAN COOPERATIVE

7–9 Florence Street, Brunswick, Melbourne, Australia

**Breathe Architecture
2007–13**

Australia is a nation of coastal dwellers, living mostly in single-family houses on the extreme edges of a barren continent. Only now, with a new surge of immigration, Asian investors driving up prices, and the growth of major cities, has urban apartment living begun to compete with suburban sprawl. Few top architects have paid much attention to this typology, but one pioneer is Jeremy McLeod, who established his practice, Breathe Architecture, in 2001. It is located in Brunswick, a northern district of Melbourne, which McLeod describes as "industrial, run-down, and dirty. It's a melting pot of migrant activity—Italian, Greek, Turkish, Lebanese, African— all coming together in one totally imperfect community." There, he lives and works in the Commons, a mixed-use block he designed for a consortium of five other architects.

The Commons comprises twenty-four apartments on four levels over a café and wine bar at the front, with bike storage and studios for Breathe and another tenant in back. It replaces a decrepit warehouse, whose paint-sprayed bricks were recycled as a colorful mosaic in the lobby. "The design strategy was to build more with less," says McLeod, "to give space and height, light and air. We realized that architects

were shut out of most development, and that we would have to fund this ourselves. The intention was to create a prototype that was sociable, sustainable, and affordable. We wanted to connect to the community."

The site borders a commuter rail station that links Brunswick to downtown Melbourne in fourteen minutes, so Breathe chose to save A$750,000 by eliminating underground parking. Zig-zag panels of opaque fiberglass, which have a long life and are locally manufactured, are set forward from the west façade. They create a thermal chimney, which also moderates heat gain and train noise. The building is set back 3 ft (1 m) to add plantings along a heavily trafficked bike path, and deep-set slit windows admit light. The south side is clad in ironbark, a very hard Australian timber that lasts at least fifty years without oiling or painting, and should hold its color. The north side receives the most sun, and the fully glazed apartments are set back behind balconies 6 ft (1.8 m) deep and screened in summer by wisteria that climbs up suspended chains. Thus, the Commons responds to the climate and (according to McLeod) is the first zero-carbon building in Australia.

The interiors put the same emphasis on frugality and inventiveness, with a succession of small moves that give the block its character. Services are treated as found art, rather than as something to be concealed. The sprinkler system is a prominent feature in the lobby, while copper plumbing, black cloth conduits, silver ducts, and red fire pipes animate the exposed concrete slab ceilings, giving each apartment added height. White walls alternate with exposed structural concrete; floors are of reclaimed and waxed Tasmanian oak. Lift lobbies are battened in blackbutt (an Australian hardwood) and mild steel, and there are two internal light wells.

Residents meet on the roof deck, where they can tend their own gardens and socialize. In the lobby, the sprinkler system and bricks from the warehouse that formerly occupied the site are treated as found works of art.

Apartments range in size from 540 to 810 sq ft (50 to 75 sq m), with generous private decks. McLeod characterizes his fellow occupants as a lively mix of creatives and retired professionals who like the idea of being part of a small community. Residents cultivate their own gardens on the rooftop terrace, which brings them together to exchange gossip and enjoy views of the city. "The sense of camaraderie that has already developed here is incredible," says McLeod, "and I think architecture has been the catalyst."

Construction was halted by the recession, but the project was bought and completed by Small Giants, an ethical investor that puts its money into social projects. That ensured the Commons' integrity, but Breathe has had a hard time replicating its success. Melbourne has a strong design culture with a great many entrepreneurs, but most of the talent and investment are directed into high-end condos. Developers are profit-driven and risk-averse—here, as elsewhere. McLeod wanted to build a similar block across the street from the Commons, but planning permission was refused after a wait of fourteen months. He hopes that small investors may join forces to promote similar developments in the future, appealing to a growing market of younger people who have lived abroad and seen how rewarding apartment living can be. Meanwhile, he is working on a larger project in Sydney where there is a 10 percent FAR (floor area ratio) bonus for the winners of design excellence competitions.

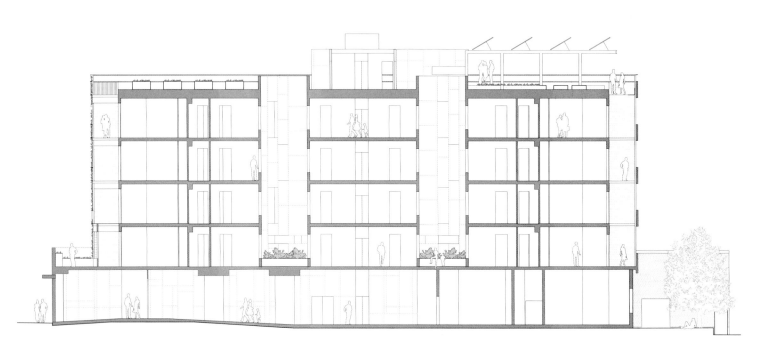

Opposite (top) and below: Wisteria shades decks on the sunny north side, while natural materials and exposed services give the apartments their informal character. Opposite (bottom) and below (bottom): Section and sample floor plan.

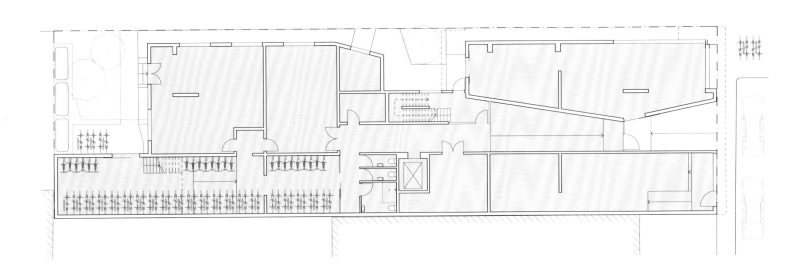

STAR APARTMENTS: ROOFTOP REFUGE

240 East 6th Street, Los Angeles

Michael Maltzan Architecture 2011–14

The Star Apartments are Michael Maltzan Architecture's third project for the Skid Row Housing Trust in downtown Los Angeles. In contrast to the firm's New Carver Apartments (pages 152–3), a sleek white cylinder with sharply faceted bays, Star is a rough-edged, asymmetrical stack of prefabricated units rising from a single-story podium of retail spaces. It is a brilliant model for future development, but it illustrates the challenge of experimenting in LA—something that baffles hidebound bureaucrats and contractors.

"From the start," Maltzan explains, "this was to be a prefab building because the Trust wanted to do a mixed-use project in Skid Row. Though they had enjoyed greater success than other non-profits, their SROs [single-room occupancy units] had been criticized for failing to participate in the life of the city. A retail facility gave them a presence on the street, but that left us with a very confined site and we needed to build quickly and less invasively." However, as Maltzan quickly discovered, it was fifty years since prefabrication had last been employed for multiple housing in LA. The Building Department considers a prefabricated unit to be a product, just like a light fitting or a door knob, and requires stringent testing and a research report when it is employed for anything larger than a single-family house. So the architects had to work closely with city authorities to develop this as a pilot project in order to secure a building permit and certificate of occupancy.

Maltzan's office designed the units, which are a uniform size and were mocked up and fabricated by a firm in Idaho. They are self-supporting and were shipped as pairs with a connector that was sawn through before they were craned into place and bolted together. Their weight is supported by a concrete deck and columns below. The wood boxes are fully equipped, and the logical course would have been to express the individual units to create a boldly articulated complex, as Moshe Safdie did with Habitat in Montreal (pages 18–19). Maltzan decided to give them a stucco finish to disguise their factory-made character. "I was afraid it would appear as though we were warehousing the homeless in containers," he says. "What would be architecturally juicy for market-rate housing would have tricky connotations for an SRO." From a bird's-eye perspective, Star does read as a constructivist assembly; close-up, it is more subdued.

The housing trust intended to keep the existing retail to generate revenue, but the LA County Health Department wanted to locate its first storefront healthcare facility here, in an effort to get involved with people on the street and address problems before they become acute. Its facility occupies half the ground floor, with parking to the rear, and offers healthcare for this and neighboring trust properties.

Star Apartments are also an experiment in densification, and in this respect, too, they point the way forward. Community areas totaling 16,000 sq ft (1,486 sq m) are located on the second floor, with tightly clustered 375 sq ft (35 sq m) living units accessed from narrow walkways above. This allowed the architects to provide an expansive deck,

Prefabricated modular units are stacked above the roof deck of an existing one-story retail block. They give a hundred of LA's homeless an opportunity to rebuild their lives.

with gardens, a kitchen, a basketball court, and a jogging track around the perimeter, in close contact with the street. The contrast of spaciousness and compression accentuates the virtues of each. One could imagine a new layer of the city, one or more stories up from the ground. For the homeless, it is literally a step up from the street. Some have been out there so long that they can no longer navigate the social network. "Shifts of scale are the hallmark of a city," observes Maltzan. "In New York, you might go from a small apartment to Central Park. I wanted to get away from the monotony and privatization of space you find in the suburbs, which have no density."

Sadly, this ambitious project is undercut by poor detailing. The budget was reduced during the recession, construction was delayed, and the contractor was out of his depth. On the plus side, Maltzan overcame many obstacles, the building is fully leased, and the tenants are happy. The housing trust has won praise, and developers have toured the project in search of fresh ideas. It may prove the seed of a new multi-level downtown, adopting prefabrication on a large scale to save time and money, and exploiting the many single-story buildings that flank the historic core.

Compact units encourage residents to socialize in the communal rooms, terraces, and garden that overlook the street. The spacious lobby (above, right) is flanked by a clinic, a parking lot, and an administrative office. Below and opposite, bottom: Plan of ground level and section.

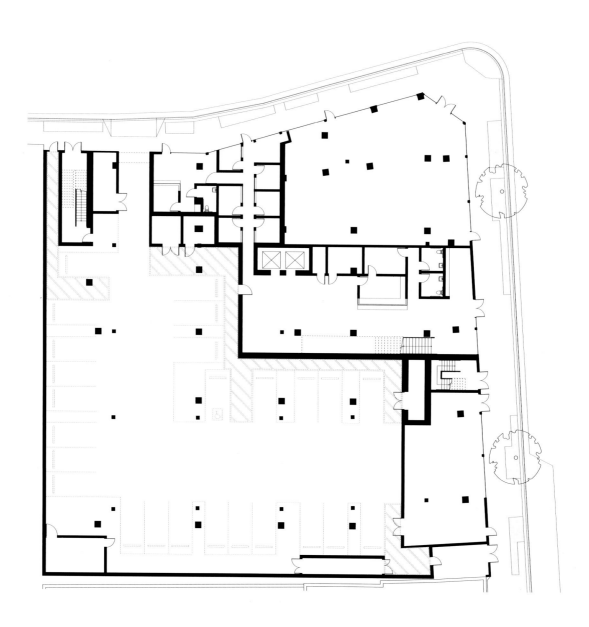

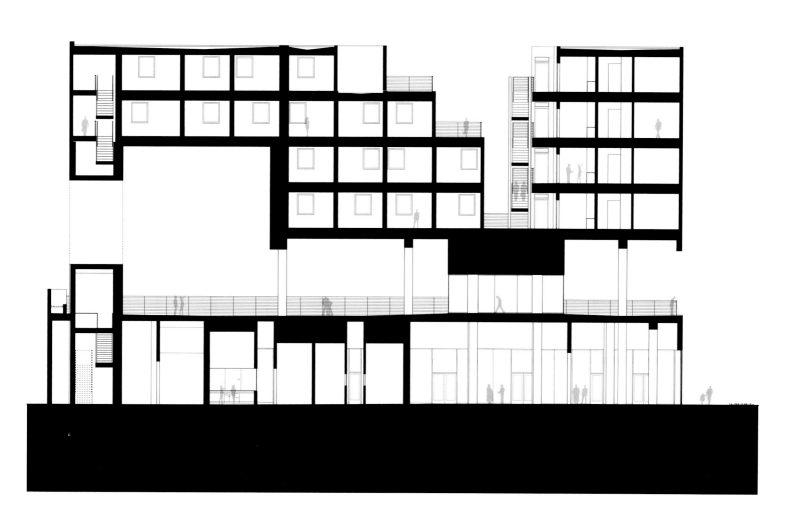

TORR KAELAN: SYNERGY AND SUSTAINABILITY

416 13th Street, San Diego, California

Rob Wellington Quigley, FAIA 2012–14

Rob Wellington Quigley is an architect with a mission. He led the way in creating humane SRO blocks for the homeless in his adopted city of San Diego. As an activist and urban pioneer, he has helped to reinvigorate depressed neighborhoods, creating live–work spaces for himself and others. "When I first moved to Little Italy in the 1970s, it was a ghost town at night," he recalls. "I was the first architect to build there since the war. Others followed, and gradually redevelopment took hold. Franchises displaced the artists and small businesses. When Starbucks arrived, I left." He bought a narrow plot in the gritty East Village area and built a five-story courtyard block that would house his office, a 2,000 sq ft (186 sq m) apartment for him and his family, and leasable space to generate income. It is a model of how much can be achieved on a small footprint and a limited budget, and it promotes a sense of community among its users while reaching out to the neighbors (which include two SROs and the new Central Library that Quigley designed).

Kathleen Hallahan, Quigley's Irish-born wife, made her debut as a contractor on this job, and in her honor he named it Torr Kaelan—the Gaelic for rock outcrop plus their daughter's middle name. Old wood-framed structures to either side posed a fire risk, so the whole building is masonry, with concrete columns and slab floors. There are shear walls to meet the seismic code, infill of concrete blocks, and joinery of redwood salvaged from the shack that formerly occupied the site. The street façade is sharply cut away and animated with cantilevered balconies. The courtyard provides access to parking garages on either side and hosts parties and neighborhood events. Above are two levels of glass-fronted studios—for Quigley and a couple of design firms—and a pair of duplex apartments on the upper floors. "On a larger site we would have added ground-floor retail," says Quigley. "The synergy of mixed-use buildings is what creates a vibrant urban environment. Thirty years ago I had to get a special permit to live over my office; now it's officially encouraged, but banks still frown on it and are reluctant to make loans."

Some of the earliest buildings in San Diego were adobe courtyards built by the Spanish settlers who colonized what is now California. Quigley likes to give his buildings a strong sense of place, reaching back for historical precedents and taking advantage of the benign climate to promote indoor–outdoor living. In designing this building, he spent a great deal of time studying the impact of light on living and work spaces, adding a yellow wall to reflect the late afternoon sunlight. It is also a model of sustainability, which approaches net zero. The thermal mass of the concrete and the expansive glazing reduce the need for heating, and rooftop photovoltaic panels often generate more electricity than the building uses. The California drought has finally persuaded authorities to permit the recycling of rain and gray water. The double-height living room in the Quigleys' apartment has an efficient Rumford fireplace, and an oculus to pull in light and act as a thermal chimney. All the garages have electric chargers.

To create affordable housing over the past thirty years, Quigley eliminated everything that was not in the standard building repertoire, relying on good construction and generous spaces. For Torr Kaelan, he indulged his love of well-crafted details. He tapped into the local pool of design talent (including graduates of two architectural schools who chose to become artist-artisans) to fabricate a flying staircase of perforated steel that links the two office levels, as well as many other features, including handrails, cabinetry, and the steel shelves at one end of his living room. The concrete blocks in the public areas and around the elevator have "juicy joints," in which the grouting oozes out and catches raking shadows from the sun—a reference to the commercial vernacular of the 1950s.

"Choreography is one of the architect's best tools, but most apartment buildings are static, poorly lit, and confining," says Quigley. He is now facing the challenge of translating the ideas he has explored on a small scale to a ten-story apartment project containing several hundred units in Long Beach, a port city south of Los Angeles. His goal there is to break open the box, pulling fresh air and natural light into every apartment and the corridors, and adding decks that are as large as the budget allows.

Two office levels (opposite, top) are linked by a perforated steel
staircase. The owner's duplex (below) opens onto a spacious terrace.

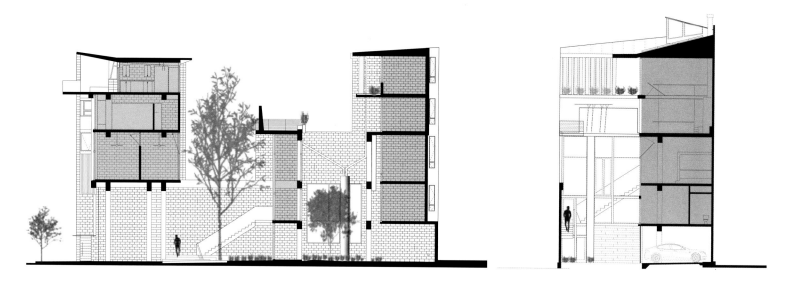

This page: East–west and north–south sections, and plans of the fifth, fourth, and ground floors. Opposite: Protective masonry walls part like a stage curtain to create a visual link to the street.

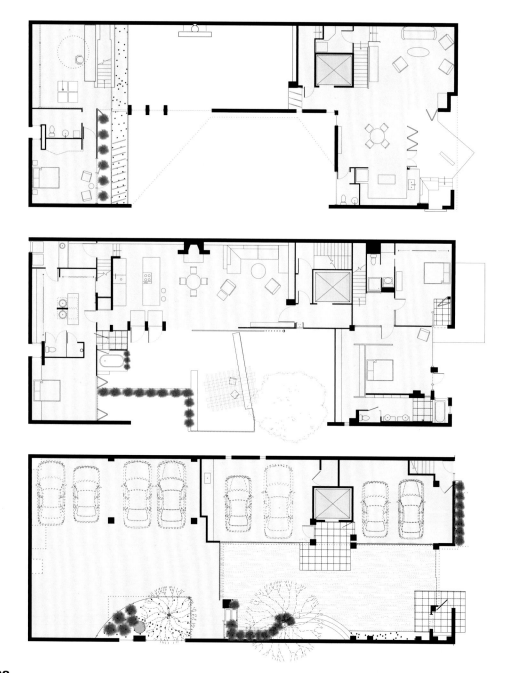

HÉROLD: ORGANIC TRIO

123 Blvd Sérurier, 19th Arrondissement, Paris

Jakob + MacFarlane
2003–08

Brendan MacFarlane is a New Zealand–born architect who relocated to Paris and established a partnership with Dominique Jakob. The firm is best known for its public and commercial buildings, notably the Docks of Paris on the Seine, the Orange Cube and Euronews (a green cube) in Lyon, plus FRAC in Orléans. Each of these is a local landmark: boldly sculptured, brightly colored or metallic, an architectural showpiece. By contrast, the Hérold social housing on the northeastern edge of Paris is softly molded and irregular, deferring to old trees and mandatory setbacks, and its goal is to build community among residents and neighbors rather than to make a splash. A hundred apartments are contained in three organic blocks of warm-toned concrete, oriented toward the southwest, and screened from a busy street by trees and a wall of excavated rocks. Each block engages the other and the ash, chestnut, lime, and plane trees that were preserved during construction. There are two levels of underground parking. The project is a model of sensitive, sustainable development, and the landscaping by Cap Paysage is exemplary.

"You cannot touch the French architectural profession more profoundly than when you build social housing," says MacFarlane. "It goes to the very core of their being, because almost everyone has lived in such apartments." All the top talents—including Christian Portzamparc, Jean Nouvel, and Édouard François, as well as the Basel-based Herzog & de Meuron—have designed notable projects, and state-subsidized housing is available to 80 percent of the French population. In the postwar years, huge high-rise blocks were built in the poor neighborhoods around the city to resolve a crucial housing shortage, but many of these have deteriorated and become immigrant ghettos, isolated and crime-ridden. Lacaton & Vassal rehabilitated one such block with notable success, but the sheer scale of the problem defies easy solutions. The new administrative entity of Greater Paris aims to break down the socioeconomic barrier between the historic center and the outskirts by enlarging the city's boundaries (as Berlin did in the 1920s) and building smaller blocks of social housing in many different arrondissements.

Hérold makes a modest contribution to that ambitious goal. The gently angled façades and tapered profiles give the buildings a welcome sense of place in a rather bleak neighborhood. After the competition-winning design had been completed, the architects realized that the tapered concrete walls and projecting terraces were remarkably similar to the bookshelves they had designed, several years earlier, for the Florence Loewy bookshop in the 7th arrondissement. Hérold's developer, RIVP, was willing to spend a little more to add amenities and create a variety of configurations. Ten ground-floor apartments are reserved for disabled residents who used to live in the hospital that formerly occupied the site. Their accommodations have resin floors, and their doors open directly into the garden. A school, a crèche, and a retreat for the elderly occupy part of the site.

Three blocks of social housing on the northern edge of Paris are richly landscaped and designed to optimize natural light and ventilation. Trasparent ETFE curtains (opposite, bottom) can be drawn to enclose balconies, and porous stone tiles provide a mossy edge that echoes the greenery beyond.

There are about eight apartments on each of the five to six upper levels, ranging in size from 270 to 810 sq ft (25 to 75 sq m), each with a different plan. There are no interior corridors; rather, the units are accessed from a service core and a short terrace to the rear. Each block is wrapped with 6 ft (2 m) deep balconies, giving the buildings a feeling of depth and increasing the usefulness of a feature that is too often a cosmetic addition. The outer edges of the balconies beyond the metal balustrade are clad in porous stone tiles and planted with moss to provide a green edge with drip-feed irrigation. A transparent curtain of ETFE (a tough material developed for marine use) is suspended from a ceiling track within the balustrade, and can be drawn to give every resident a winter garden that makes the outdoor space usable year-round, by absorbing heat from the low sun.

The architects claim that Hérold is one of the first sustainable apartment buildings in Paris. Most of the apartments have a double orientation, and those facing north have smaller windows and a higher level of thermal insulation. Rainwater gathered from the roof is recycled to provide 60 percent of the building's needs. Rooftop solar panels provide heat for two-thirds of the water used in the bathrooms.

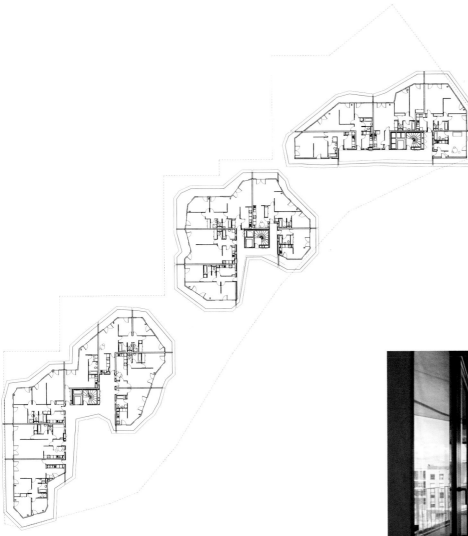

Gently angled forms and generous plantings make these buildings
a welcome presence in a rather bleak neighborhood. Above and below:
Sample floor plan and section.

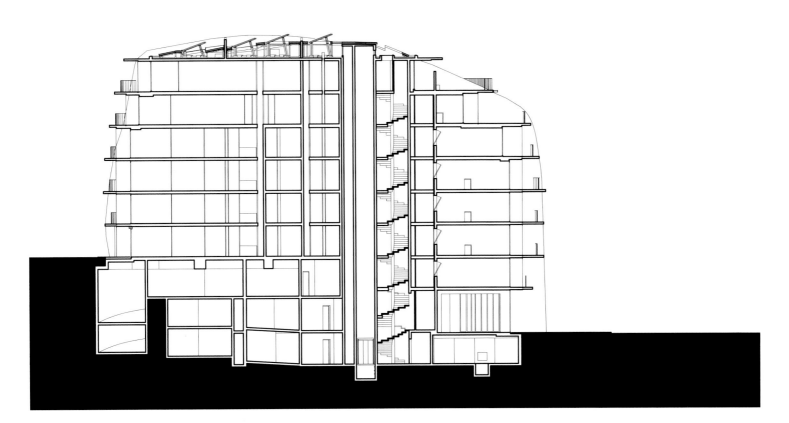

SONGPA MICRO HOUSING: MAXIMIZING THE MICRO

Songpa-dong 9-17, Songpa-gu, Seoul

Single Speed Design
2012–14

Jinhee Park was born in South Korea and worked there as an industrial designer before moving to the United States to study at the Harvard Graduate School of Design. After graduating with a Master in Architecture, she formed a partnership with her compatriot John Hong, who had spent most of his life in America. They opened Single Speed Design in Cambridge, Massachusetts, in 2003, followed by a satellite office in New York and another in Seoul. SsD designed several houses in Massachusetts before partnering with a developer in Seoul to create Songpa Micro Housing. On a tightly confined site in a residential district, it has created a springy, silvery enclosure that offers an intriguing mix of private and shared spaces.

There is a critical shortage of affordable housing in Seoul because so many Koreans want to live in the fast-expanding capital, which has been voted the most livable city in Asia. In 2008, the city authorized micro-apartments as small as 130 sq ft (12 sq m)—since revised to 150 sq ft (14 sq m)—to accommodate a growing number of singles. As Park notes, "Historically, that's a new phenomenon: Korea is very family-oriented and young people would continue living with their parents until they married and started their own families. The government offered tax benefits to promote construction of micro-apartments and a few architects got involved, but most developers took advantage of the law to pack even more people into a block and create a bad living environment."

The client for Songpa was an art-loving doctor who owns several hospitals and shared the vision of SsD, so the project became a cooperative venture. "We researched the concept and the needs of single people in the hope that this could be the prototype for a new model of housing," says Park. "We wanted to improve the quality of life, even though the individual units are minimal, and to make a fresh start." Although the architects understood that the complex would probably have the strongest appeal to young people who live without a lot of possessions and enjoy hanging out together, they wanted to appeal to a broad public and bring flexibility to a rigid housing market.

Height and setback rules were strictly enforced. The building is elevated above ground-level parking, making it appear to float among its stolid neighbors. The architects liken it to a delicate flower in the urban jungle. Stainless-steel louvers are twisted to provide a privacy screen and brise-soleil that wraps the building while revealing the buzz of activity within, especially at night. Steps lead down to a basement café. Sixteen modular units were assembled from concrete panels on site and slotted into six upper floors. They are configured in an irregular fashion that allows some units to be combined while leaving generous shared areas and bridges spanning an open space at the center. The separation contributes to sound insulation, along with the triple glazing that shuts out street noise. Each unit is equipped with the essentials for living, including a Murphy (pull-down) bed, a washing machine, and a stovetop. A clerestory supplements the window and provides even lighting.

SsD's project is a model of communal living and a demonstration of flexibility. When the client saw how well it was turning out, he had the units on one floor combined as an apartment for his daughter, and those on the first floor as an art gallery. Other units have also been joined together, reducing the number and diversity of residents and the building's social impact. But the basement continues to serve as a café, toy store, and stepped theater, and there has been positive feedback from the people who do live there. They make good use of the shared spaces, drop into the café for breakfast, and get around the city by bicycle or public transport, with no need of scarce parking spaces.

The architects are interested in developing their concept on a larger scale. "We could create a similar community in a sixty-unit block," says Park. "Big corporations like Samsung are interested in the idea, but we have to educate them to work on a smaller scale than they are used to. Even for them it's hard to assemble a large lot. And it's essential we retain control to ensure that the concept is not misused." Therein lies the challenge that confronts all idealistic architects. In every other field of design, successful prototypes go into production, the unit cost tumbles, and almost everyone can share the benefits. Yet each innovative housing project is an isolated effort and there are almost no economies of scale.

A tiny complex of micro-apartments, each fully equipped and opening onto shared spaces, offers a model for larger developments. The stepped basement (opposite, bottom) doubles as a theater and a toy store. Below and bottom, right: Elevation and section.

The New Carver Apartments (see also opposite) look out onto an elevated freeway in downtown Los Angeles.

Michael Maltzan Architecture was founded in 1995, and is based in the Silver Lake district of LA. Its principal focus is on cultural and residential buildings that engage the public.

MICHAEL MALTZAN

HOUSING FOR ALL

Crest is a block of single-room apartments raised over a landscaped parking area. It was commissioned by the Skid Row Housing Trust for a site in North Hollywood.

"I've always shared the early modernists' belief that housing is the fundamental typology in architecture because it's a microcosm of our lives, public and private, and the city. Because of that, we approach every project with a similar level of design intensity. A house for a wealthy person has a different set of parameters than housing the homeless, but the fundamentals are not that dissimilar.

"Each of our four projects for the Skid Row Housing Trust [in Los Angeles] has been an evolutionary step in the trust's thinking about the ingredients of such housing and its impact on the city. We've learned a great deal about the functional needs, and that has shaped our designs. Each has been a laboratory test of how a community can grow and thrive in an individual building and what architecture can do to support that community—a piece of a much larger project about housing and the city.

"We understood when we did the Rainbow Apartments—our first for the trust—that most of the people who would be living there had spent such a long time on the street that they had built a defensive shield to protect themselves in public spaces, and had lost the ability to socialize. Architecture can help with but not solve such basic social issues. We were able to create a semi-public place that had the potential to work therapeutically. More single-loaded corridors and gathering spaces, which invite residents to navigate a semi-public realm as a first step towards resuming a public life.

"The driving force behind the New Carver Apartments was the trust's ambition to meet the challenge of homelessness in LA as a whole, not just on Skid Row. Their concern was that if all their buildings were located there, it would balkanize the district, much as the postwar projects did. They wanted a site that was visible and intertwined with the city, so they picked a lot adjoining the 10 Freeway that is one of LA's prime public spaces. At Star [page 128], the goal was to create a mixed-use building that would participate in the street life of the city. That had a big impact on the way our design was developed.

"For a community to grow, a feeling of collective ownership is important, and the Star gardens have had an extraordinary effect in promoting cooperation and stimulating a conversation about healthy eating that didn't exist before. At Crest, the fourth building, the garden enjoys parity with the architecture. It occupies a long, skinny site in North Hollywood—a suburban context that's quintessentially LA. There are homeless people across the entire city, not just in downtown. In contrast to the typical dingbat apartments with street-level garages, the four-story, seventy-unit block is raised on concrete columns above a landscaped ground floor that can also be used in part for parking. The building feels as though it's floating above a garden.

"There's a burning need for more housing at almost every income level, especially low to moderate. It's going to take leadership in many areas. There has to be a stronger political commitment to building more housing and incentives to private and non-profit developers. The process of getting entitlements has to be streamlined, and we need to relax zoning requirements and allow residential construction on sites that are presently off-limits. Star Apartments demonstrates the potential for multi-family modular construction—and the more that gets to be built in that way, the more positive the effect on the cost, quality, and rapidity of building.

"Non-profit developers think about projects in a different way from profit-driven developers, who see buildings as product. Product is evaluated by what is in the marketplace. It's not driven by a deeper investigation of needs. SRHT deals with rapidly changing issues and finds the right programmatic mix for an underserved market. That allows for a lot more invention; it's not a question of budget, but one of ambition."

Each unit at the New Carver Apartments opens onto an inner courtyard, a space ideally suited to socializing.

SPIRIT OF PLACE

Every great city is a palimpsest of streets, buildings, and open spaces that mark its evolution and serve its users. Landmarks are set off by the lesser buildings in between, the scale and spacing is lively but humane, and there are places for everyone to live, work, and play. That ideal is rarely achieved, and it is becoming ever more elusive. Too much regulation can cramp the organic growth of a city, while unfettered private development will overwhelm it.

Architects are called upon to perform a balancing act, designing buildings that will stand out and fit in, even though they may differ sharply from their closest neighbors. Paris is justly celebrated for its layering of old and new, with the Eiffel Tower—fiercely denounced when it was first proposed—as a graceful vertical accent, and the universally despised Tour Montparnasse as a solitary eyesore. All other high-rises have been banished to the periphery. Few other cities achieve this combination of harmony and distinction; too many have sold out to the highest bidders.

The spirit of place is an elusive commodity: a fusion of topography and architectural history, streetscape and skyline, as well as the intangible rhythms of daily life. New York and San Francisco view themselves as uniquely urbane, each in its own particular way. David Adjaye, an African turned world citizen, researched the DNA of Harlem before designing Sugar Hill, a building that subtly references the local vernacular and the rich history of the neighborhood. At the opposite end of Manhattan, Neil Denari responded to the industrial past of the High Line with a machine-like structure of polished steel that swells out over the former tracks to command views in every direction.

In San Francisco, where every intervention is tightly controlled, Stanley Saitowitz created a linear block of apartments that highlights a point of entry to the city. Dramatic in its sweep and unabashedly contemporary in its expression, Octavia picks up on the color, materiality, and façade treatment of its neighbors, reinterpreting historical styles in an inventive way.

The sprawling metropolis of Berlin may have striven too hard to assert the Prussian values of order and discipline as it reconstructed the dead zone that formerly divided the city. A chief planner was determined to turn the clock back a century and succeeded only in hobbling some of the world's best architects. Ironically, Jürgen Mayer benefited from the constraints in designing an infill block of upscale apartments, toning down his customary exuberance to respect the street and enrich the living environment.

No such challenges confronted Henning Larsen Architects when it designed the Wave: a free-standing waterfront complex that gives the provincial Danish city of Vejle a memorable civic icon. It could easily have been an empty gesture—form over function—but the apartments fit snugly within its fluid curves. Here, the inspiration came not from the city but from the hills and water that frame it, resulting in a building that takes its cues from nature.

SUGAR HILL: NEIGHBORHOOD RESOURCE

155th Street at St. Nicholas Avenue, New York

Adjaye Associates
2012–14

Harlem is one of the poorest neighborhoods in New York, sharing Manhattan Island with the greatest concentration of wealth in the world. First developed in the 19th century as an exclusive white suburb, it soon acquired a new identity as a mecca for African Americans migrating from the South. The historic Sugar Hill district nurtured the Harlem Renaissance of the 1920s, an outpouring of music, literature, and art, and an expression of racial pride. Rising rents are making the area less affordable, while gentrification of the handsome old houses is strengthening its appeal to outsiders. That is the context for the creation of Sugar Hill, a mixed-use development by the non-profit Broadway Housing

Communities (BHC). Drawing on thirty years of innovative building and programming, BHC commissioned David Adjaye to design a landmark building that would house the needy, invigorate the neighborhood, and express the spirit of place.

"We tried not to make something merely acceptable to the poor—I find that idea quite offensive," says Adjaye. "Too many social housing projects have a single purpose. What excited me was to create a building that was not just about housing [but rather] a new urban experience." He and his associates researched the history of the neighborhood and worked closely with the client and community to develop their design. A thirteen-story slab of apartments cantilevers out on two sides, rising from a podium containing an early childhood education center, with a children's museum of art and storytelling in the basement. Entered from a landscaped plaza, and visible from all sides, it is a massive structure, clad with precast concrete panels that are tinted charcoal and ribbed to catch the light. The long north and south façades have a serrated profile that echoes the stepped façades of the row houses on adjoining streets.

In lesser hands this somber-toned block could have seemed oppressive, even sinister; instead, it is a beacon of hope. The concrete sparkles in the sunlight and a subtle pattern of roses emerges—surface ornament created by putting a vector drawing into the formwork. Sugar Hill is

The stepped façades of Sugar Hill (right) mimic the Harlem row houses nearby. A subtle pattern of roses emerges from the ribbed and pigmented concrete (above).

located in the Heritage Rose District, and the flower has long been a feature of Harlem. The sharply angled façades and shifted masses reduce the apparent bulk of the building. It takes advantage of its steeply sloping site and its location on the highest point of the island, which commands a 360-degree panorama, from the World Trade Center tower far to the south, up to Central Park, and beyond to the north where the Hudson and Harlem rivers converge. Natural light spills into the museum from above. The education center has expansive glazing that puts the children in touch with the bustle of city life and the trees in a neighborhood park. At the upper levels, Adjaye aimed for what he calls a "jazz composition of windows of different sizes," which frame views and pull in abundant light. Terraces on the second, third, and ninth floors promote social exchange, and the sunken courtyard to the south serves as a play area for the children.

The interiors are frugal but equally inspiring. Working on a tight budget, project architect Marc McQuade and his associates were able to give every room a feeling of spaciousness. There is a wide variety of accommodations, from 500 sq ft (46 sq m) studios to 1,200 sq ft (112 sq m) three-bedroom apartments, as well as community rooms, offices for BHC, and a workshop where residents can create

An early childhood education center opens onto a narrow courtyard (below). The building serves the local community and animates this residence for low-income and homeless New Yorkers.

and exhibit their own artworks. That ties in with the museum, which shows work by local artists and children, as well as hosting an artist in residence. To appreciate the impact this building has, it is essential to understand how great is the need for affordable housing and community services. Seventy percent of the units are reserved for families earning less than half the average mean income in New York, and twenty-five are set aside for individuals and families who are currently in the city's homeless shelter system—which has been widely decried for its lack of humanity and security. In a video produced for the *Architectural Review*, Adjaye explains his intentions, but it is the interviews with residents that capture his achievement and move one to pity.

"We received about 48,000 applications for the 124 units," says BHC director Ellen Baxter. "The need is so great we could build many more, and we hope this model sets an example for other neighborhoods to create integrated facilities, using the capital that's available to build affordable housing and stretch it to provide other community benefits."

This page: The interior of the education center, and saxophone-playing resident James Rooke. Opposite: Sample floor plan and section.

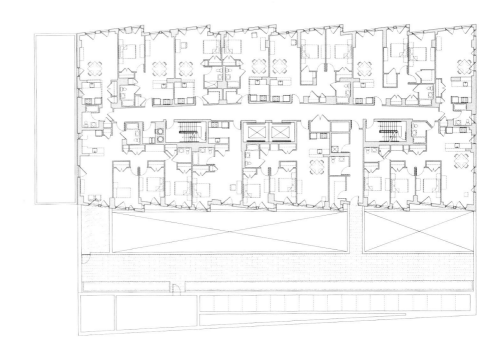

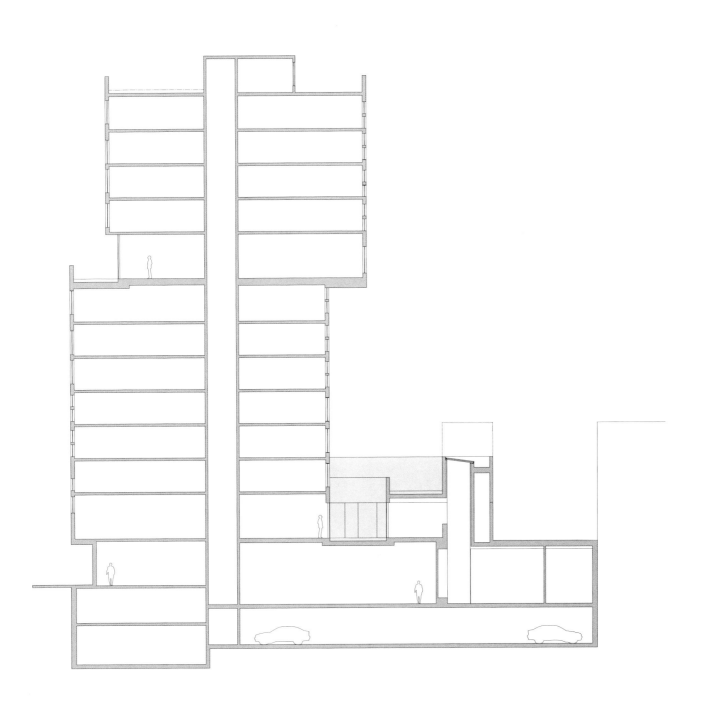

THE WAVE: FLOWING ASHORE

Ved Bølgen,
Vejle, Denmark

Henning Larsen Architects
2003–09

The waters that separate the Danish islands are usually calm, but two tall waves have washed over the waterfront of Vejle, a small city on the eastern shore of Jutland. Like many former industrial centers, the municipality is trying to rebrand itself as a progressive hub of culture and high tech, cleaning up its harbor and setting high standards for new development. That prompted a local investor to hold a design competition for the apartments he planned to build on a prominent waterfront site. Inspired by his father, who had built an Art Deco lido that was a sensation in its day, he aspired to create a new civic icon. The 2003 competition attracted 500 entries. PLOT, a partnership of Bjarke Ingels and Julien De Smedt, proposed five towers spelling out the name of the city, "VEJLE"—much like the Hollywood sign. It was rejected as impractical and because it could be read from only one side. Henning Larsen Architects edged out other fanciful schemes with the Wave, a design that reads well from every direction and celebrates the maritime spirit of the city.

Like Jørn Utzon's Sydney Opera House, the project evolved from a rough conceptual sketch. In the forty years since that masterpiece limped to completion, most Danish architects have played it safe. In the early 2000s, they began to burst out of the box, and the Wave is a product of that newfound exuberance. "In creating these soft shapes, we took our cues from the ocean, clouds, and the rolling hills behind the city," says project architect Søren Øllgaard. "We saw them as a romantic depiction of the Danish landscape, and divided the 150,700 sq ft (14,000 sq m) of habitable space into five ten-story towers that would work individually and as a single complex, while opening view corridors to the water from the city. We resisted the idea of making the waves different sizes—that would have seemed too much like a joke."

What gives the Wave its special distinction is the subtle asymmetry of the forms, which are expressive yet harmonious. Viewing them across the water, from the bridge that spans the harbor or the motorway that flanks the city, they seem to grow naturally from the land as a fusion of solid and liquid materials. In the initial design, the twenty-one apartments in each block were to be accessed from a central service core and exterior terraces. The developer insisted, however, that people paying a premium price would demand greater privacy; thus, the terraces were eliminated, and twin cores provide direct access to each unit. The exterior walls are clad in white porcelain tiles that are self-cleaning and project forward to shield the glazed façades and give the complex a sharp edge. Metal louvers screen a podium of parking.

Although the shapes have a child-like appeal, the blocks have attracted older buyers. The apartments are long and narrow, and extend through the block with 8 ft (2.5 m) deep balconies that offer sweeping views of the harbor and the lush countryside. Sloping side walls pierced with horizontal slit windows give residents a feeling of protection that complements the transparency of the ends. Apartments vary in size from 860 to 1,615 sq ft (80 to 150 sq m), with

2,700 sq ft (250 sq m) duplex penthouses beneath the peaks of each block. Every surface is impeccably crafted and detailed. Although the planned café and meeting room were eliminated, the residents share a strong feeling of community. The scheme was voted the best multiple residential building of 2010 by a jury of European architects.

Regrettably, the Wave fell prey to cost overruns. The developer was carried away by his enthusiasm and bought the 100 × 660 ft (30 × 200 m) site from the city at an unreasonably high price. Only two of the five towers were built, and that helped to drive up construction costs to 40 percent over conventional buildings. Vejle has only 60,000 inhabitants, so it proved hard to sell the expensive penthouses. For the architects, it was a mixed blessing: they were invited to participate in many competitions but had a hard time getting housing commissions because clients were afraid that they would design another version of the Wave. Only now are there plans to build the remaining three towers.

Ironically, this may be the last free-spirited project for a while. "The financial crisis dampened the spirit of innovation in Denmark; we are back to sober and orthogonal designs," says Øllgaard. The Danes do that better than almost anyone else, and it may be as well for Vejle that the Wave remains a singular extravagance.

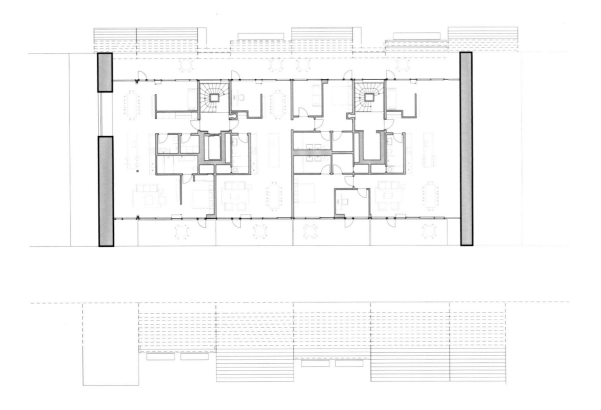

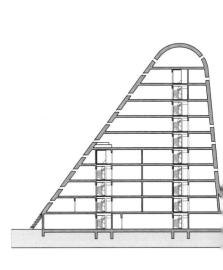

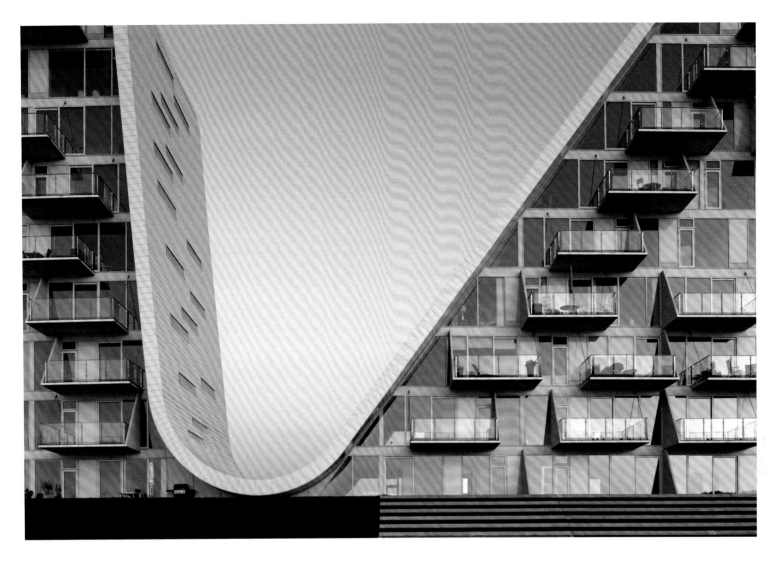

Each apartment has balconies at front and back looking out to water and green hills. Five "waves" were planned for this Danish port (see section, below), but only two have been realized. Opposite, bottom: Sample floor plan.

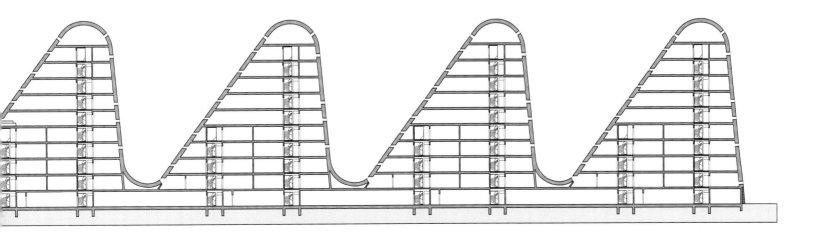

8 OCTAVIA: ABSTRACTING THE CITY

8 Octavia Boulevard, San Francisco

Stanley Saitowitz/Natoma Architects 2013–14

San Francisco grew out of Gold Rush frenzy in the mid-19th century—a grid of mansions and slums sprawling over the hilly terrain—and evolved into a tough port city. In the postwar years, as industry declined and the docks relocated to Oakland across the Bay, it succumbed to gentrification and became narcissistic—regulating every aspect of design and closing the door on innovation. Alfred Hitchcock's *Vertigo*, a movie shot on location in 1957, captures the dream-like sense of unreality that still enchants the city's votaries. The Loma Prieta earthquake of 1989 was in some respects a blessing in disguise, providing an opening for exciting new buildings by Herzog & de Meuron, Morphosis, and Renzo Piano, besides dooming the elevated freeway that disfigured the waterfront. A second gold rush of high-tech fortune seekers has reinvigorated the former industrial zone south of Market Street, driving property prices sky-high.

Stanley Saitowiz has exploited that openness to new ideas and the urgent need for more housing, designing about thirty apartment buildings in the Bay Area since 1991. No other architect has so successfully abstracted the DNA of San

Francisco, creating blocks that reference the traditional urban fabric without mimicking its period style. A prime example is 8 Octavia, located on the boulevard of that name in the Hayes Valley neighborhood. When an elevated section of Interstate 101 was torn down, a skinny site was created alongside the busy surface street. To fill it, Saitowitz designed a linear block that provides a bold introduction to the city as motorists come down to earth.

"Every exterior begins with the character of the site and here we took our cue from an ornate Victorian façade on a neighboring corner," says Saitowitz. "In contrast to its ornamental green façade, ours is a machine that residents can manipulate. Traditional San Francisco façades are pretty, with delicate vertical articulation, but contemporary buildings need to protect and temper us with a minimum of energy. Their skins have to be alive, breathing and changing with the time of day and seasons, responding to variations in climatic conditions." That translates into vertical louvers, set into 18 ft (5.5 m) wide bays, which each resident can individually adjust. They animate the long, west-facing street front, creating a constantly changing billboard. Originally they were to be glass, but that was changed to green-painted aluminum, which dissolves into the windows and plays off the exposed concrete frame.

There are forty-nine apartments, ranging in size from 740 to 1,740 sq ft (69 to 162 sq m), on six floors above street-level retail and basement parking. Ceiling heights are set by a non-negotiable height limit on buildings in San Francisco, but the floor-to-ceiling glazing makes rooms feel loftier and more spacious. Saitowitz negotiated with the city to waive the requirement for a back yard and incorporate the same area in four light wells, two cut into the street front, the other two internal. By dividing the space and threading it through the building, he was able to increase the exposure of each

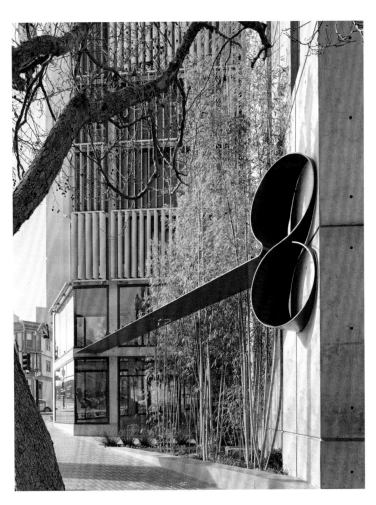

In their color and scale, the new apartments at 8 Octavia Boulevard abstract the older buildings of San Francisco. All open onto light wells carved out of the skinny block.

apartment and pull in more natural light. That creates pockets of tranquility and eliminates corridors: each apartment is accessed from an outside terrace, which promotes casual encounters among the residents.

Saitowitz himself was able to design the open-plan apartment interiors, with their exposed concrete ceilings and hardwood floors. He likens them to urban lofts that enable residents to organize their lives as they wish. Two-bedroom L-plan apartments wrap the vertical voids on two sides, and services are compressed into a thick wall on one side to free up the rest of the floor area. To achieve the same flexibility in space planning in the one-bedroom I-plan units, the kitchen is located in a pod on one side, the bathroom on the other. At the top of the building, the Ls and Is are combined to form three-bedroom units with spiral stairs leading up to private rooftop terraces.

Inevitably, apartments of this quality command high prices, but Saitowitz recently completed a project in San Francisco's Mission District where the market rates are lower, in addition to prefabricated modular housing for students in Berkeley, California, and projects across the country. (For the architect's insights into the design of apartment buildings and his suggestions for increasing their quality and quantity, see the interview on page 196.)

Below: Services are compacted so as to create open-plan living and kitchen areas. Each resident can adjust the aluminum louvers to regulate sunlight. Opposite: Section and sample floor plans.

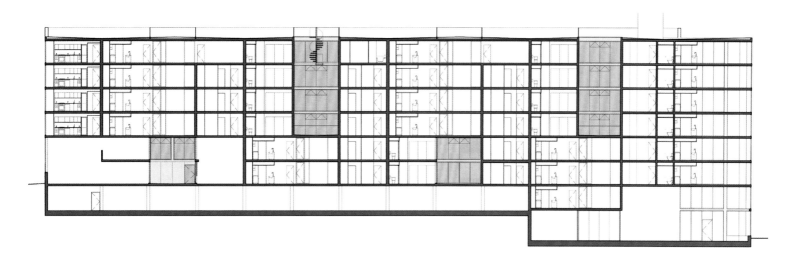

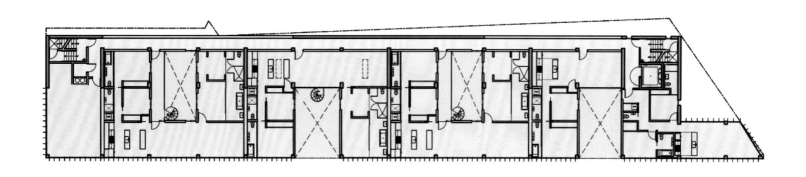

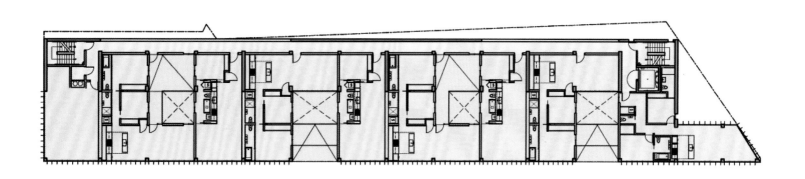

THE ALEPH: UPDATING HISTORY

Petrona Eyle 355, Puerto Madero, Buenos Aires

**Foster + Partners
2006–13**

Spanish settlers laid out Buenos Aires on a grid according to the Laws of the Indies (the body of law used by Spain for the government of its colonies), and this sprawling metropolis of 14 million still clings to its legacy of master-planning and the stately edifices of its heyday in the Belle Époque. Paris and Madrid have been the models for generations of architects, and the tide of innovation that swept over Brazil and Uruguay from the 1930s on scarcely affected Argentina. Tradition rules within the Porteño establishment, inspiring Juan Bautista Frigerio, who heads the BA office of Foster + Partners, to draw upon historical models in designing the Aleph, a nine-story concrete-frame block of high-end apartments with an enclosed garden to the rear.

The Aleph is located in Puerto Madero, adjoining the financial district. British investors developed the district as a port in the 1880s, but the docks have moved further out. The city established a corporation to master-plan the area, and Alan Faena, a leading local developer, had the vision of creating an upscale mixed-use community, which he named the Faena Arts and Technology District. He started by commissioning Philippe Starck to turn a vintage warehouse into a hotel, and, over the past decade, the neighborhood—especially the waterfront—has become a lively mix of new towers, shops, and adaptive reuse of old structures. In 2005, Faena invited the Foster office to design several buildings, but only the Aleph has thus far been realized. The national economy is lagging, and Faena has redirected his attention to Miami.

Faena's demands for the Aleph were simple: make it functional, sustainable, and unique, without going over budget. Frigerio had designed residential projects for other firms, and welcomed the opportunity of doing another with the Foster team. To give it a distinctively Porteño quality, he reinterpreted two features of the local vernacular. The wave

of poor Italian immigrants that flooded into BA in the late 19th century had to build their houses on narrow plots, so they took the Spanish courtyard model and cut it in half. These long, thin houses were nicknamed *casas chorizo*, and many survive. The other feature was the *boveda*: a bowed brick ceiling vault resting on cedar beams. In the Aleph, the *casa chorizo* reappears in the form of lofty screened terraces that supplement spacious balconies and allow residents to take advantage of the benign climate. The *boveda* is recreated as bowed ceiling vaults of fair-faced concrete. There are fifty apartments over ground-floor shops and cafés, basement parking, and service areas, plus a rooftop infinity pool.

As in all of this firm's buildings, there is a crisp authority that is entirely modern in spirit, even as it references the past. The sliding louvered sunscreens that shade the terraces and the floor-to-ceiling glazing have their counterpart in the slatted shutters, short balconies, and tall windows of Beaux Arts houses in BA. The lyrical rhythm of the vaulting complements the orthogonal geometry of the block and evokes the water a short distance away. Smaller apartments of about 960 sq ft (90 sq m) are located on the first four floors, larger units of 1,616–2,370 sq ft (150–220 sq m) on the next four, and a 6,460 sq ft (600 sq m) penthouse fills the ninth.

Foster + Partners had the great advantage over most architects of designing the minimalist interiors itself, and many of the apartments were customized. The layouts reflect the growing informality of upper-class living, in which the kitchen and dining room are no longer segregated and the interior spaces flow freely. There is a warm palette of bronzed windows and sunscreens, wood balustrades, and stone tiled floors. Every room has a window, and bedrooms are separated from bathrooms by glass sliders, which make both feel more spacious. Another device was to tilt up the underside of the balconies where the glass wall meets the ceiling, which opens a view of the sky and makes the interiors seem to expand. The larger apartments face north and south, and have a separate entrance to their patios. The feedback from residents has been positive—as Lord Foster discovered when he visited the property and was invited into several apartments.

The success of the Aleph has inspired several copycats, and Frigerio would love to bring the same skill set to the design of affordable apartments, but cautions that it would have to be on a large scale to cover the office overheads. His mixed-income master plan for the city of Rosario is currently under construction, and one could imagine the impact that a similar Foster scheme would have in the capital.

Opposite: Undulating concrete ceilings evoke traditional *bovedas* while giving the spacious apartments the character of a loft. Below: Sample floor plan and section.

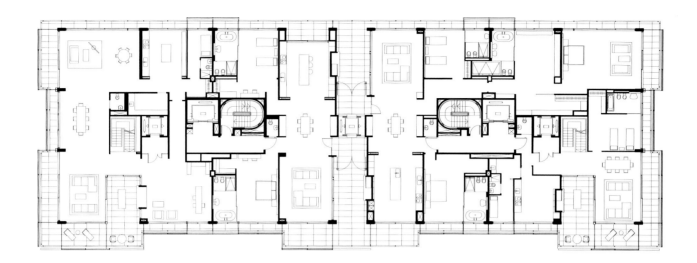

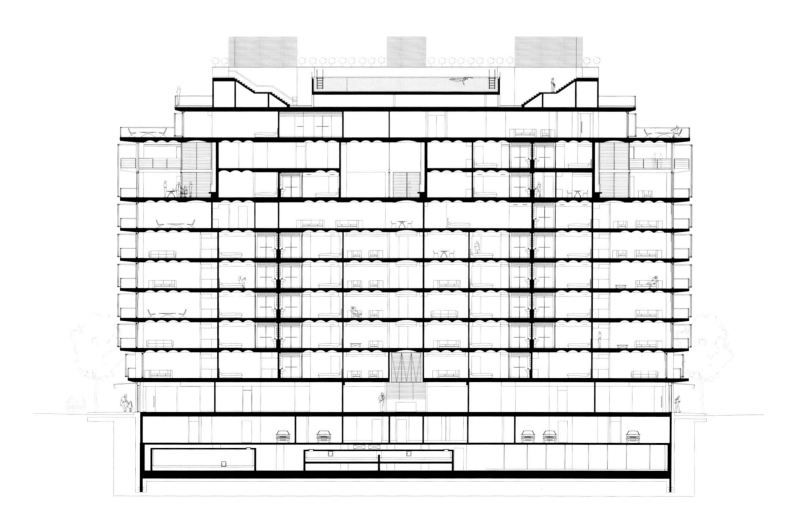

HL 23:
LEANING IN

515 W. 23rd Street,
New York

Neil M. Denari Architects
2005–13

The High Line—an elevated freight track in Lower Manhattan transformed into a linear park—offers rustic illusions and thrilling views of the city. It may soon be walled in by generic blocks, but there are still vistas of the Empire State Building, over the low-rise blocks of Chelsea and the West Village, and down to the harbor. Jean Nouvel and Frank Gehry make fleeting appearances on the Westside Highway. The one significant neighbor is HL 23, a fourteen-story condo block sheathed in glass and steel, swelling out over the park. It was Neil M. Denari Architects' first ground-up building and it demonstrates how New York's tough zoning code can be turned to advantage.

"It's easier to break out of the box in the Wild West of Manhattan," says Denari. "This is still unsettled territory, with large warehouses and few residents to raise objections." That will soon change as the area gentrifies, but two first-time developers seized their chance to exploit a tiny site alongside the High Line before the park opened, and commissioned NMDA to design something radically new. In spring 2005, the architects produced thirty schemes in six weeks, pushing the envelope to create a block that would have an elegant signature while maximizing square footage and relating harmoniously to the park. "It had to fit in and stand out," explains Denari. "The design was developed from the inside out, in an accumulation of small negotiated moves. We wanted the form to be a continuous surface rather than the conventional wedding cake with set-back floors." In fact, it is stepped out and back, with a middle section that is cantilevered nearly 6 ft (2 m) over the park to the east, and again to the south over a spur in the tracks.

That sculptured form was submitted to the city planning department for prior approval, and it granted seven of eight requested waivers in the hope that this block would set a benchmark for future development. Such a complicated building takes time to prepare and construct. Two years were required to secure all the permits and locate manufacturers that could meet precise specifications within the budget. The large triple-glazed façade panels with slender stainless-steel mullions were imported from China, the structural steel from Canada, the ribbed steel fascia from Argentina, and the black anodized aluminum that conceals the rooftop services from the UK. Unforeseen delays and a quest for perfection prolonged construction over four years, but the developers—Alf Naman and Garrett Heher—held firm.

Most New York residential buildings have concrete frames; HL 23 uses steel to support the cantilevers. The peripheral cage of steel beams is fully exposed and protected with fire-resistant paint. To dramatize their presence the diagonals extend through three or four stories, and the concrete floor plates are exceptionally thin, making the building appear taller and lighter. A ceramic frit projects the structure onto the curtain walls so that the diagonals are visible from the outside even when the motorized window shades are lowered for privacy or sun control. Each fritted outline is different, and the corners are rounded to soften the sharp angles. This gives the façade a depth and a dynamic quality to which the eyes and the body react. The fluid profile is enhanced by the play of light across the east wall, which is clad in molded bead-blasted steel panels. There are four patterns, configured differently to suggest greater diversity.

Luxury resides in the volumes and natural light of this building, as well as in the materials and precision of the detailing. In the all-white lobby, Denari designed a cantilevered reception desk that was hand-carved from a single block of marble by an Italian sculptor. There is a two-story maisonette with a private garden at the base, and a duplex penthouse with an upper-level room that opens through glass sliders onto a wraparound terrace. Each of the nine apartments in between occupies a floor and is subtly different in plan and height. Thomas Juul-Hansen, a Danish architect who formerly worked with Richard Meier, designed the minimalist interiors with their oak floors and figured marble bathrooms. But, to a greater degree than in most upscale condos, it is the architecture that counts. The angled planes of glass frame the sky, distant towers, and the foreground of water tanks, as well as the lush plantings along the High Line. Inside and outside are as one; residents and outsiders share a private monument that helps to shape the public realm.

One of the first and best residential towers to exploit the green
promenade of the High Line in lower Manhattan, HL 23 rises from
a small footprint and extends out on two sides.

Below (bottom right) and opposite: With one apartment on each floor and expansive glazing, HL 23 enjoys a 270-degree panorama over the city and the Hudson River. Below (left and right): Section and sample floor plan.

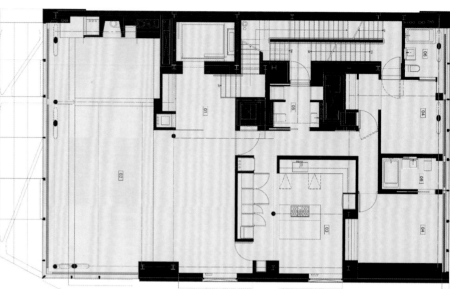

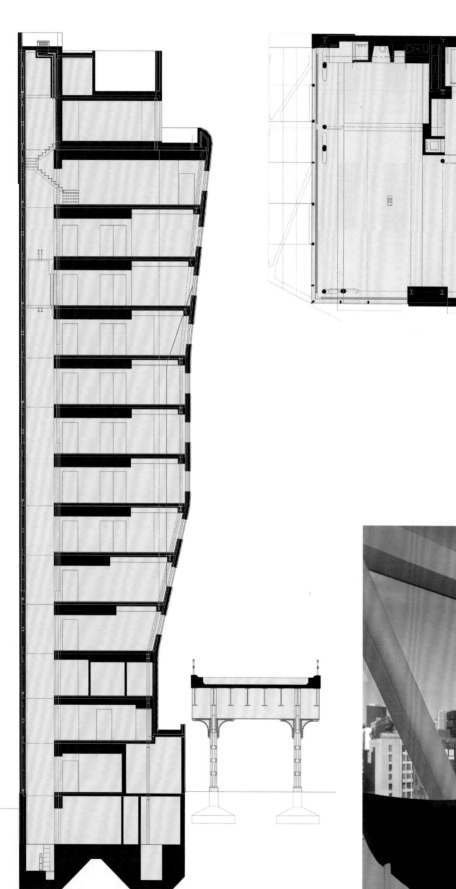

JOH 3:
LAYERED FAÇADES

**Johannisstrasse 3,
Berlin**

**J. Mayer H.
2008–12**

Devastated by war, sundered and isolated during the Cold War, Berlin has recovered some of the allure it enjoyed during the Weimar era. East of the Brandenburg Gate, the historic monuments of the Mitte district have been meticulously reconstructed, and new buildings must conform to strict constraints. Jürgen Mayer, the free-spirited principal of J. Mayer H., had to rein in his sculptural impulses in designing an upscale apartment building on a confined site near Museum Island. As he explains, "Berlin authorities are still very controlling, though things are beginning to open up. The requirements are not as strict as they used to be—you no longer have to clad half the façade in stone, except in specific

locations." The architect of the Seville Parasol and several follies in Georgia concedes that "it's sometimes good to have a framework."

The client for JOH 3, named for its street address, was Euroboden, an ambitious Munich-based developer that has set a lead in hiring top architects—including David Adjaye and David Chipperfield. This was its first project in Berlin and, because of the location, it held a competition for the design—an increasingly common practice in private commissions that allows developers to consider alternative ideas. Although the area is central and was master-planned twenty years ago, it is only now being redeveloped from the ruins and vacant ground that East Germany bequeathed. JOH 3 is located on a narrow street and looks out over a car park that will soon be built up by Herzog & de Meuron.

Mayer took his cues from the classic Berlin courtyard block, and most of the twenty-three spacious apartments on the upper six stories are oriented toward the southwest, facing inward over the verdant private garden. Office spaces occupy the ground floor, and there is a narrow paved light well planted with bamboo. The distinctive feature of the block is the carapace of aluminum extrusions that frame the expansive street-front windows, admitting light and views while providing shade and privacy. They are reprised as balustrades on the garden façade, and Mayer carefully calculated their height to provide a privacy screen without imposing an oppressive barrier. These lamellae add a depth and rich play of shadow to the façades. The parapets of the walls that retain the two courtyards evoke some of the architect's love of baroque exuberance, and the surface patterns will eventually be covered with greenery.

Berlin was a great bargain in the decade following reunification, but prices have steadily risen as more affluent settlers have joined the bohemians and creatives who pioneered its renaissance. The city is still less expensive than Munich, Hamburg, and other provincial German capitals, but the impact of the recession persuaded the developer that it needed to offer more design features in order to sell the apartments, and so the budget was increased. Mayer exploited the trapezoidal site and the irregular garden to give every apartment a distinctive plan. Sizes range from 590 to 960 sq ft (55 to 90 sq m), while the two penthouses were combined to create a single 5,920 sq ft (550 sq m) condo that opens onto roof terraces. The apartments are linked by staircase/elevator cores at either end. To enrich the interiors, sunken living rooms are defined by built-in seating, and open onto expansive balconies looking out to the green wall. Sale prices ranged upward from 5,000 euros per sq m (11 sq ft), and occupants include a DJ, a gallerist, a curator, and a political consultant. Many are self-employed, and they have considered buying one of the storefronts to turn it into a club and meeting room for residents.

Mayer himself has lived in an old apartment building for the past twenty years, and he recently completed another, more affordable block in the industrial city of Jena. Like most architects, he would prefer to build more affordable apartments, but rising land prices make it hard to do so. He praises the alternative approach of the *Baugruppen*, the cooperative ventures that have flourished in Berlin. As he explains, "Fifteen years ago architects without work would buy land, produce a design, and find people who wanted to live in an urban community. Or it started with people pooling their resources and then hiring an architect." It makes good sense to cut out the middleman, and it is a model that deserves to be widely copied. However, the need to achieve a consensus among people who are committing their savings and have different preferences can produce good living environments that are architecturally bland.

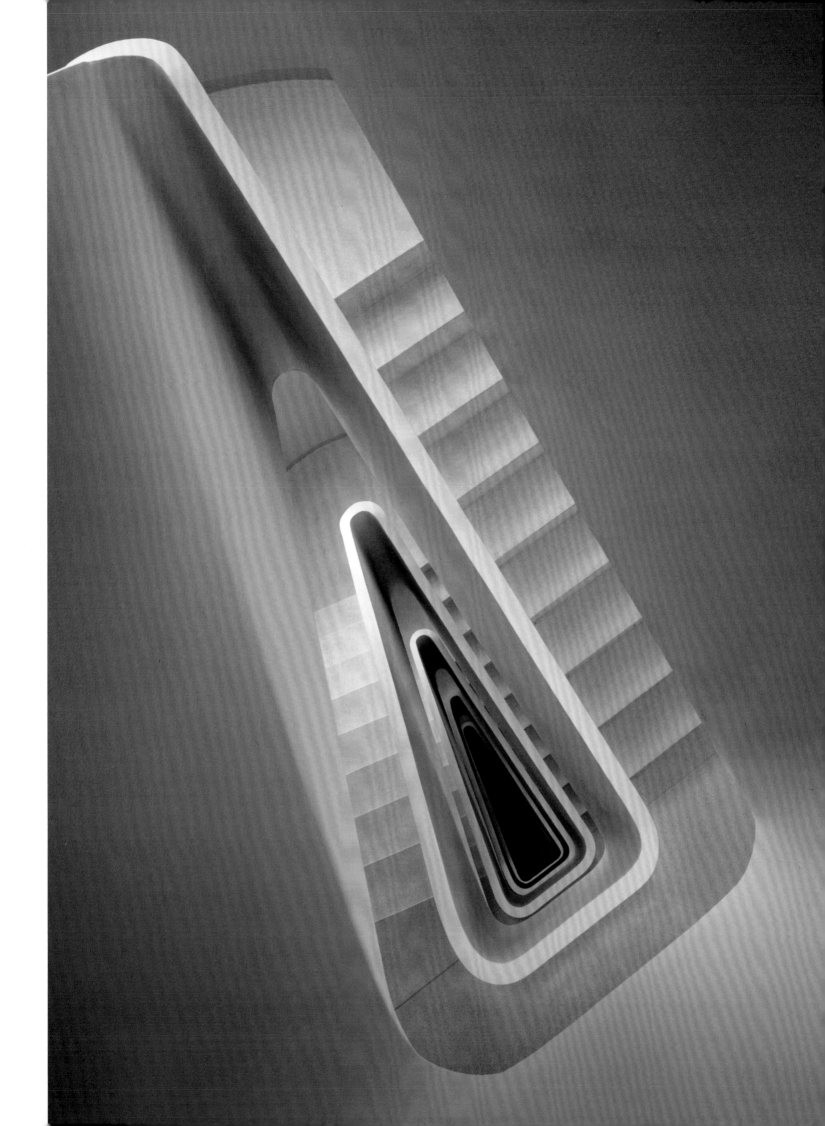

Sample floor plan (below) and section (opposite, top). The developer increased the budget in order to provide the apartments with a greater range of design features (below, bottom, and opposite, bottom).

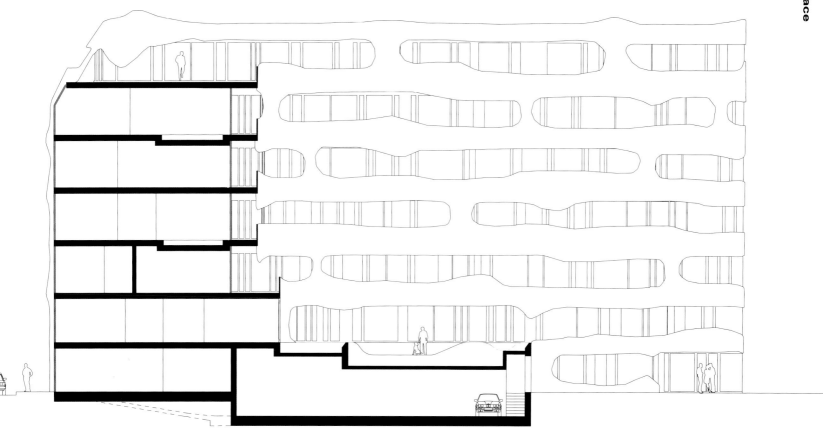

Stanley Saitowitz/Natoma Architects was established in 1980 in San Francisco. It has completed more than thirty apartment buildings in the city, in addition to houses and other projects in the Bay Area and across the United States.

STANLEY SAITOWITZ

RIGOROUS STRATEGIES

A deep block is sliced in two, and metal louvers reference the clapboarded façades of traditional houses in San Francisco.

Yerba Buena Lofts, a larger-scale reinterpretation of historical models, is located in the former industrial zone South of Market.

"Over the past twenty years, our emphasis has shifted from designing single-family houses in the country to multi-family blocks in San Francisco, and now country-wide. Context is still the point of departure. The DNA of this city is a product of geography and geometry. At moments it looks like Mykonos— white cubes climbing the hills. Most of our work is located South of Market [SoMa], where there's a mixture of one- and two-story industrial buildings alternating with residential. The context is not as 'postcardy' as other parts of the city. It's an area where the City Planning Department has encouraged development and we don't encounter as much neighborhood resistance to our buildings.

"The first building we did in San Francisco was a live–work space on Natoma that is now our office. We did two more infills on the same street, and these were the laboratory for developing all the principles we've been applying in our urban housing since then. Doing these buildings myself demonstrated that they were economical and offered a lot of quality.

"The big developers don't care about design. We work for smaller firms who do care, which is why they hire us. Our buildings look more expensive than they are because we have rigorous strategies on how the money gets allocated. Our plans are very methodical and repetitive: well-developed templates for the layout of units. We compact all the services into pods or a thickened wall. The loft is our prototype for the contemporary urban apartment—the most square footage with the fewest walls. Everyone has the same requirements, regardless of income level, so you give people as generous an allowance as possible. However, light wells bring greater benefits than a few extra feet of floor space.

"Yerba Buena Lofts [2004] on Folsom comprises 200 units in an 86 ft [26 m] high block. All the apartments are double-height with a mezzanine bedroom, contained within a 16 sq ft [5 sq m] module that is expressed in a grid of concrete fins on the glazed street façade. Each bay is divided vertically with translucent horizontal channel glass on one side, clear on the other side around the balcony. Our goal was to flip the horizontality of the neighboring workshops and express it vertically. We wanted to relate to the tradition of bay windows but in a contemporary and restrained way.

"The building where I live is two blocks away at 1234 Howard, an eighteen-unit block that I developed with two partners in 2008. It abstracts a Jack and Jill, a typical San Francisco building type, in which a staircase runs up the center between two bays, creating a three-part division. Here, we sliced through the block to create a light corridor, with bridges that link the apartments on each level to the elevator. A drive runs under the light corridor to access street-level parking. The horizontal metal louvers were inspired by traditional clapboard façades and complement the verticality of the block. These are genetic elements that make up the character of the city.

"Dealing with the City Planning Department, which doesn't understand architecture, is a very slow process; we sometimes wait three times as long to get a permit as it takes to build. We have a lot of trouble with the preservationist spirit in that department, now that almost every district of San Francisco is considered historic and every new building has to comply with its character. We firmly believe in respecting scale; Planning wants textbook replicas.

"Far too much of our effort goes into explaining what we are doing. The bureaucracy is obstructive, and committee-type negotiations tend to make the buildings worse, not better. The only people who benefit are the banks because of the carrying costs on land—and the consumer pays. As a result, housing in San Francisco may be more expensive than in New York. Everything is getting absorbed at ridiculous prices. Only if the market slows is there likely to be an incentive for better quality."

REACHING SKYWARD

We don't know what the floor area ratio was for the Tower of Babel, or whether it received a permit, but its failure dampened the demand for high-rise buildings right down to the 19th century. It was the development of steel-frame construction, electricity, and the elevator that made possible the towers of Chicago, New York, and metropolises around the world. Frank Lloyd Wright proposed a mile-high tower that could probably be realized with today's software programs. Even without technology, it is possible to live high off the ground. In Caracas, the half-completed shell of the Torre David was occupied by squatters who established a lively community up to the twenty-fifth floor before they were compelled to move on.

The urge to build higher, driven more by the search for status than profitability, seems to go in waves. There is currently a building boom in Manhattan and London that may peter out, leaving only an inchoate mix of high-rise follies and a few new landmarks. In the Gulf States and China, the frenzy has been uncontrolled and one wonders if there are enough fat cats to fill those luxury condos in the sky. Steven Holl has designed three megastructures—Linked Hybrid in Beijing, Horizontal Skyscraper in Shenzhen, and Sliced Porosity in Chengdu. Each is an attempt to create a vibrant, mixed-use community within intimidatingly vast cities.

They and the examples that follow break out of the box that imprisons most apartment dwellers. The gains of living high are swiftly erased when sweeping views are blocked by other towers as formulaic as one's own. "Cities are increasingly dense, vertical, and shaped by developers, not civic vision," declared Ole Scheeren in an address to the World Architecture Festival. "The spaces between towers are unconsidered, and that should inspire a fresh approach." He was speaking of Asia, but Western cities are heading in the same direction.

Frank Gehry long wanted to build a residential skyscraper and finally got his chance in New York, on a site bracketed by two blue-chip monuments: the Woolworth Building and the Brooklyn Bridge. He has created a worthy neighbor, whose gleaming folds enhance the skyline while embracing a lively mix of living spaces. From Beijing, Ma Yansong reached out to a satellite of Toronto to realize his first building outside China. A sensuously twisted tower of small apartments, it was quickly dubbed Marilyn Monroe, and proved so popular that a sibling was built alongside.

Marco Polo is a new landmark by Behnisch Architekten on the redeveloped waterfront of Hamburg: a tower that disappears behind a flourish of balconies, flaring out to add living space and command sweeping views. In São Paulo, Brazil's overbuilt metropolis, Studio MK 27 has created V_Itaim, a modestly scaled tower that far outshines its corpulent neighbors. A developer in the Cypriot capital of Nicosia commissioned a tower from Jean Nouvel, and it is aptly named White Walls for the dazzling concrete façade, lightened by pixelated openings and abundant plantings. In Singapore, Moshe Safdie has reinterpreted Habitat, his debut project in Montreal, in twin towers that step back and are linked by recreational spaces at three levels.

8 SPRUCE STREET: SHIMMERING SHAFT

8 Spruce Street, New York

**Gehry Partners
2003–11**

The elevated walkway of the Brooklyn Bridge is an ideal vantage point from which to admire the sweep of Manhattan. As you cross the East River, you can glimpse the length of the island, and, in the right light, it is a thrilling urban spectacle. Off to the left are the tightly clustered towers of the financial district; to the right is a wider sweep of high-rise offices presided over by the Empire State Building. Directly ahead are the graceful neo-Gothic Woolworth Building, once the city's tallest, and a shimmering, rippling steel tower that conducts a dialogue with that century-old landmark. This new addition to the skyline is 8 Spruce Street, the first tall building to be realized by Gehry Partners. It is located mid-block in an area with few tall buildings, and it is easy to walk past without seeing the shaft, which is more conspicuous from afar than it is close-up.

The client, Forest City Ratner Companies, wanted a signature building that would maximize revenue; the architects sought an elegant and distinctive profile. Gehry looked hard at the city's towers to get a feeling for the context, and his design is as unique and site-specific as was the Chrysler Building in 1929. A seventy-six-story tower of 900 rental units, clad in stainless steel, is set back from a reticent five-story brick podium containing an elementary school, with an indoor pool and other resident amenities on the upper level.

As project architect Craig Webb recalls, the design team explored fifty iterations, including cylindrical, cruciform, and even rotated forms—which, in a residential complex, posed problems of lining up plumbing connections. Eventually, they settled on a slender T-plan tower with an undulating steel skin and bay windows. The folds deepen towards the top of the tower, but there are enough shallow and flat plates to keep the cost within a tight budget. The surface geometry was mapped by Digital Project, a software program developed by Gehry Technologies, and the steel serves, like the crown of the Chrysler Building, as an ever-changing mirror of the sky.

"Like all our projects, 8 Spruce began with block models," recalls Webb. "We looked at different apartment types, how big they were, how they fit into the floor plate and zoning envelope. The goal was to maximize the surface area and get the best size and depth for each apartment, with as many corner units as possible, and we ended up with this plan." The developer would have preferred a block that was shorter and fatter, but Gehry insisted it had to soar. Zoning regulations require an 85 ft (26 m) setback from the street wall and a maximum diagonal dimension of 180 ft (55 m), but that left lots of room for a game of push and pull between client and architect. A landscaped entry plaza that links the streets to north and south provided a bonus that allowed the architects to add stories. "We tried a lot of schemes for the top of the building, including a cupola, which would have echoed neighboring buildings," says Webb. "But that made it too historical-referential and postmodern in character. So after considering many alternatives, we sheared the top flat."

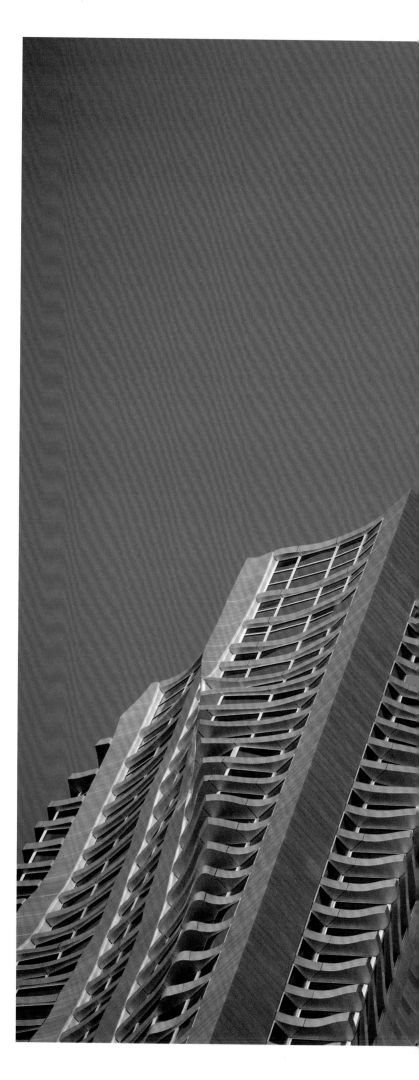

Leading architects building in New York generally design the exteriors and leave the interiors to others. Gehry insisted on designing everything, and on challenging the market-driven dogmas of the leasing agents. Most Manhattan apartments are formulaic in their layout, the size of the rooms, and the amenities. Everything is rectilinear. "At the start, we were told the walls had to be all-glass to maximize views," recalls Webb. "We said that a beautifully framed bay window is something people can relate to better than a glass wall. There was a huge fight. We were mocking up windows in our parking lot."

The struggle paid off for everyone. Gehry found ways of constructing a complex façade at a cost comparable to that of a brick veneer with punched windows, or a glass curtain wall. The alternation of shaped and flat panels, hard and soft, imparts a dynamic energy to the tower. Each apartment—ranging in size from one-room efficiencies to spacious three-bedroom units—has a distinctive plan that is shaped by the undulating skin and window bays. Most have views in two directions, even three, to provide a vista of rooftops and water tanks, or an uninterrupted panorama of city, water, and sky. Some tenants have views of a neighboring bay, and all can enjoy a seamless link with the world beyond and the constantly shifting play of light.

A boldly modeled high-rise clad in stainless steel looks out over the East River with the landmark Woolworth Building behind.

Opposite: The rippling façades of the tower and its setbacks make reference to classic skyscrapers, notably the Chrysler Building. Above: A furnished show apartment. Below: Two sections and a sample floor plan.

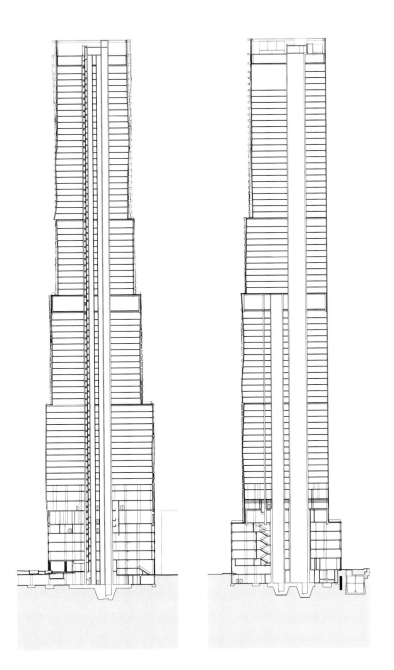

ABSOLUTE TOWERS: CHANNELING MARILYN

50–60 Absolute Avenue, Mississauga, Ontario, Canada

MAD Architects
2006–12

Ma Yansong has achieved international fame for a handful of spectacular buildings, and his rapid ascent may be a harbinger of what China has to offer the world in return for all the buildings it has commissioned from Western architects. Ma got his master's at Yale, interned with Murphy/Jahn in Chicago, Peter Eisenman in New York, and Zaha Hadid in London, and then returned to Beijing to open his own office in 2004—only seven years after the government had first permitted private firms to compete with the big state design institutes. After a rocky start, Ma secured major commissions in China and won a competition to design a residential tower in Mississauga, a lakefront suburb of Toronto that has become a major city in its own right.

The client was Fernbrook/Cityzen, a local developer that collaborated with the municipal authorities to develop five towers. Three conventional blocks had been developed, and the city suggested a competition to generate fresh ideas. Ma had been planning an organic tower in his head for several years. He quickly sketched a sinuous form that swelled and rotated, worked it up, and won the competition. The

Locals saw the sensuous curves of the first tower as a homage to Marilyn Monroe. A sibling was built to meet demand.

competing designs were exhibited and, in a popular vote, the citizenry approved the jury's choice. Officially known as the Absolute Tower, it was quickly nicknamed Marilyn Monroe; and, when all 400 units were presold in a day, Ma was commissioned to design a sibling. He agreed, on condition it be 65 ft (20 m) shorter than the 560 ft (170 m) original.

Together, these towers provide the city with the civic icon it wanted, and they have proved far more popular than the plain shafts that surround them. This should encourage other developers to take a chance on something that is out of the ordinary. For Ma, the extraordinary is the new norm. Although the fifty-six- and fifty-story towers are outwardly complex, they are supported economically by a grid of concrete shear walls. Their aerodynamic profiles allow the wind (which can be very strong coming off Lake Ontario) to pass smoothly around them—as with an airplane wing—and this stabilizes the upper floors. Curtain walls would have been too costly, so the architects used a simpler window wall system. Wraparound decks provide private outdoor spaces for every resident, and the projecting planes serve as shading devices in summer. They have also been engineered to support the weight of small trees in planters.

"The form of Absolute projects a sense of identity, but architecture needs to create a feeling of community as well," says Ma. He regrets the fact that he was not as involved in the design of the residential interiors, or of the lobbies, pool, sports facilities, and meeting spaces at the base of each tower. There are about ten apartments on each floor, ranging in size from 800 to 1,080 sq ft (75 to 100 sq m), and they are directly accessed from a central service core. The curved outer wall imparts a dynamism to the living spaces, and the glass-railed terraces extend the interiors into space, with panoramic views of the lake and downtown Toronto. Six levels of underground parking link the two towers.

The success of Absolute has helped MAD Architects win many more commissions, and it is currently developing residential towers in Toronto and New York, in addition to the Lucas Museum in Chicago and a small condo development in Beverly Hills (page 244). Ma has applied the lessons learned from his early work to major projects at home. "Chinese residential buildings, whether high- or low-cost, tend to have the same typology, with nothing to distinguish one from another," he observes. In Beijing, he has designed a cluster of thirteen twenty-four-story towers with three-story lobbies as gathering places for residents, dividing each tower into eight vertical neighborhoods. He is also trying to raise the bar on social housing in the Chinese capital, designing a low-cost, high-density project that provides a good living environment and opportunities for social interaction. "It's the first time the city has hired an architect, and they admitted they had made many mistakes," says Ma. "As an example of their thinking, they told me to specify strong doors because poor people won't open them with their hands but will kick them open."

As Ma travels back and forth from China to the United States, from costly to frugal housing by way of splashy arts buildings, he has the potential to change the way people live.

Opposite: With their dynamic forms—both inside and out—the two towers contrast sharply with their more conventional neighbors. This page: Section and sample floor plan.

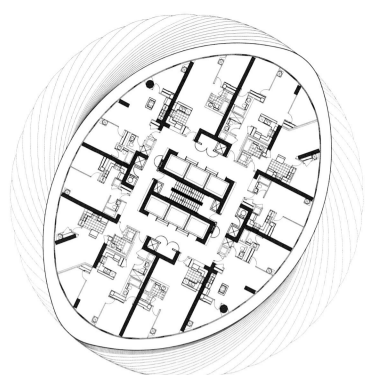

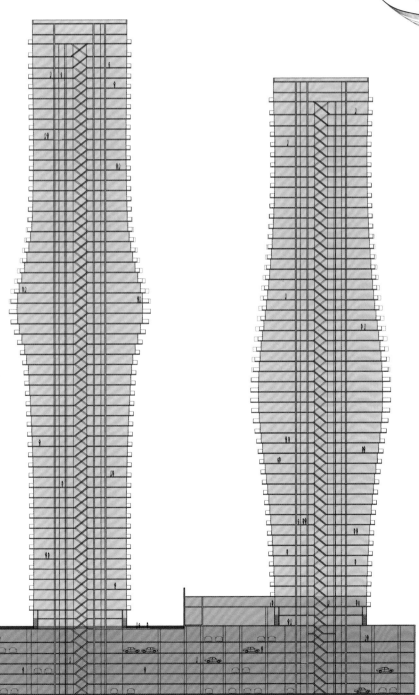

MARCO POLO TOWER: FRAMING VIEWS

Hübnerstrasse 1, Hamburg

Behnisch Architekten 2006–11

The Free and Hanseatic City of Hamburg is one of the sixteen states that make up the Federal Republic of Germany, and one of Europe's largest ports—although the docks have relocated to the mouth of the Elbe. That has freed up the former industrial waterfront for HafenCity, a mixed-use development fronting a promenade that links the old city to the new Elbphilharmonie concert hall and the cruise ship terminal. Few of the new buildings have much distinction and many seem insubstantial beside the buildings that define the city: Fritz Höger's Chilehaus (1924) and the massive brick warehouses of Speicherstadt, both UNESCO World Heritage Sites.

That posed a challenge to Behnisch Architekten, a Stuttgart firm that won a competition to design a new headquarters for Unilever and the Marco Polo condominiums on a prominent waterfront site. "It's very difficult for an outsider to work in Hamburg—it's a closed, risk-averse society," says principal Stefan Behnisch, "but a new city head of design was determined to open up the selection process. Without him, we would never have been allowed to compete. Having won, we had to persuade the developer that the office block and apartment tower were different animals and shouldn't look the same."

As built, the two are clearly distinct: the horizontal exoskeleton and transparent skin of Unilever playing off the flared Marco Polo Tower. Highly expressive, but simple and functional in intent, the design of the tower went through many different iterations—in sketches, and in physical and digital models. The concrete frame is faced with precast concrete panels and high-performance glass. "The client wanted a flexible plan so that each floor could contain a single apartment or four," Behnisch explains. "Given the small footprint, we insisted that each should have generous terraces—outdoor living spaces that looked out to the city and the harbor." The terraces' soft lines, together with the rotation of each level, disguise the rectilinearity of the tower and lighten the swelling form. Behnisch calls the wide terraces "lips," and likens the configuration to that of a ballet dancer poised on one toe. And although this architect would never lapse into literal representation, there is a clear echo of the prow and decks of a ship in the harbor.

A flared tower with wraparound balconies and light-filled lobby animates the HafenCity development that has replaced the inner-city docks of Hamburg.

In contrast to many eye-catching blocks, where interiors are shoehorned into an eccentric shell, Marco Polo was developed from the inside out. The decks serve as outdoor rooms in summer, providing privacy and shade, and protect the glass sliders from the winter storms that roll in from the Baltic. They give sun-worshiping Germans the delicious feeling that they have been transported to the Mediterranean, and turn each apartment into a house in the sky, with a front yard for plantings. Behnisch designed the tower to minimize internal structural supports and allow residents to customize their apartments. Four architects were invited to design model interiors, and four buyers selected the restrained design of Behnisch, with its stepped wood floor and cove-lit ceiling. For one owner, he went on to create a radical, space-age interior.

Germany is a leader in mandating energy conservation, and there are high standards for HafenCity. Marco Polo goes even further in achieving sustainability. Vacuum solar collectors on the roof employ a heat exchanger to cool the apartments in hot weather, supplementing the passive strategies. Innovative sound-insulated air louvers in the sleeping areas provide noiseless natural ventilation.

The developer was willing to spend about 20 percent more than is customary and give Behnisch greater freedom of expression, in order to secure an immensely greater profit. There are fifty-eight units in the seventeen stories, ranging in size from 645 to 3,660 sq ft (60 to 340 sq m), and nearly all enjoy spectacular views. For a while, these were the most expensive condominiums in Germany, fetching 12,000 euros per sq m (11 sq ft)—which is still a great deal less than their equivalents in London or New York, and has since been topped by a property in Munich. Although justifiably proud of what his team has achieved, Behnisch derives greater satisfaction from a large low-income project with a communal atrium that he completed in his home city of Stuttgart. "We have more fun doing affordable housing, provided we can work with a developer who has a conscience," he insists. "Client and tenants are usually more grateful for what you do, and more supportive."

Opposite: Spacious apartments open onto views of the city and its harbor.
In its exuberance, the tower is a worthy heir to Fritz Höger's Chilehaus.
This page: Section and sample floor plan.

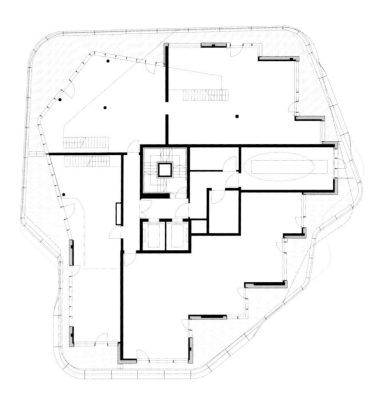

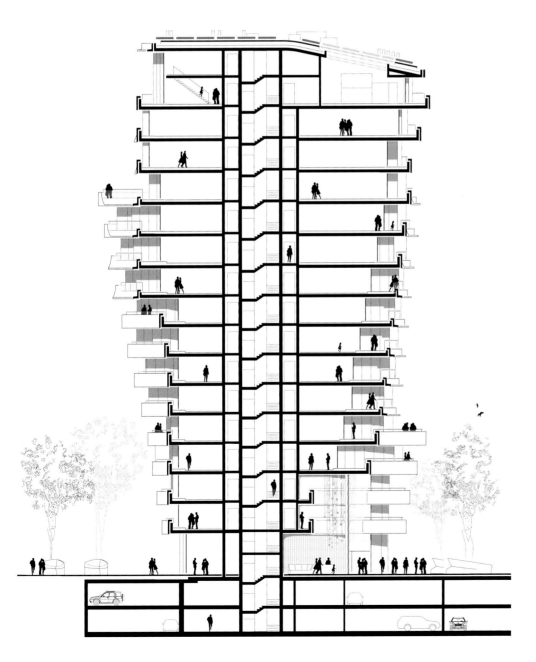

V_ITAIM:
FILTERING LIGHT

**Rua Salvador Cardoso 30, Itaim,
São Paulo**

**Studio MK27
2011–14**

São Paulo is second only to Mexico City as the largest metropolis in the Americas: an intimidatingly vast expanse of high-rises, leafy residential neighborhoods, slums, and squatters' encampments. It is a microcosm of Brazil in its extremes of wealth and poverty, with traffic so congested and crime so rampant that the very rich prefer to get around by helicopter. The city's vibrancy compensates for its many shortcomings, and it is a showcase of brutalist, mid-20th-century architecture by Paulo Mendes da Rocha, Lina Bo Bardi, and João Vilanova Artigas, as well as some organic buildings by Oscar Niemeyer. Marcio Kogan, who heads Studio MK27, is an heir to this tradition of excellence, and

his houses have a simplicity that belies their strength. Each is a response to the site, whether in the city or in the coastal zone that provides a weekend escape. Long horizontal volumes open onto shady courtyards, and there is a distinctive mix of exposed concrete and finely crafted natural materials.

Although Kogan had previously completed two small apartment buildings, it was his houses that brought him the commission to design V_Itaim, a thirteen-story tower containing ten full-floor condos and a duplex penthouse. Rising from a 6,670 sq ft (620 sq m) footprint, it is named for its verticality and Itaim, the commercial-residential district in which it is located. "Real estate companies don't usually come to architects like us—they are only interested in profit," says Kogan. "But Vitacom is a medium-sized developer that wanted to do something better and knew our work. It was a first for them, but now they are using other architects. They were willing to budget more than usual for quality materials, and it paid off. All ten apartments have sold at a premium, and the project won first prize in the São Paulo Biennale—which usually gives this recognition to a museum or other public building." Other prestigious awards have followed.

V_Itaim occupies a corner site facing east, with a bakery at the base of the north side, a ground-floor lobby, and a mezzanine gym. In its slender profile and impeccable detailing, it stands out from its larger neighbors and incorporates many

Sliding and folding shutters of perforated freijo wood animate the façades and complement the board-marked concrete floor planes of this modestly scaled block.

features of the firm's houses. Its projecting floor plates and expressive use of board-marked concrete in the walls evoke a modernist classic of the 1950s. Slender columns loft the building above the street, establishing a visual link to the small garden at the rear. Its elegant simplicity and taut geometries serve as a reminder of Brazil's golden age—before the military dictatorship suppressed progressive architects in the 1960s, driving Niemeyer and others into exile. Perforated freijo wood shutters fold or slide, shading windows and terraces while drawing in breezes and creating constantly changing patterns on the façades. There is an echo of the mashrabiya, a fretted screen that provides shade and privacy, which the Arabs took to Portugal and Spain, and which was then passed on to the Hispanic empires in the Americas. Shutters give V_Itaim its special character, the wood playing off the board-marked concrete, solid off void, with a sense of tactility and craft.

The other special quality of the tower is the generosity of the interior spaces. Each apartment is 1,400 sq ft (130 sq m), but feels much larger because its undivided living area opens through glass sliders onto a protected terrace that measures 10 × 12 ft (3 × 3.7 m) and serves as an outdoor living room for much of the year. Warm-toned hardwood floors complement exposed concrete and white drywall. The service core is located to one side, and elevators open directly into apartments on each floor. Peripheral columns support clear-span floor plates, so that internal walls are non-load-bearing and can be removed. Kogan is remodeling one apartment for a resident who wants an uninterrupted loft space.

Financial and political crises have slowed construction in Brazil, but Kogan is hopeful that he has raised the bar on apartment buildings and will secure more commissions when the economy picks up. However, water is running short in the nation's largest city and growth has to be controlled. That is a challenge that even the best architects can do little to resolve. In the meantime, Studio MK27 continues to design emphatically horizontal houses, following its venture into verticality.

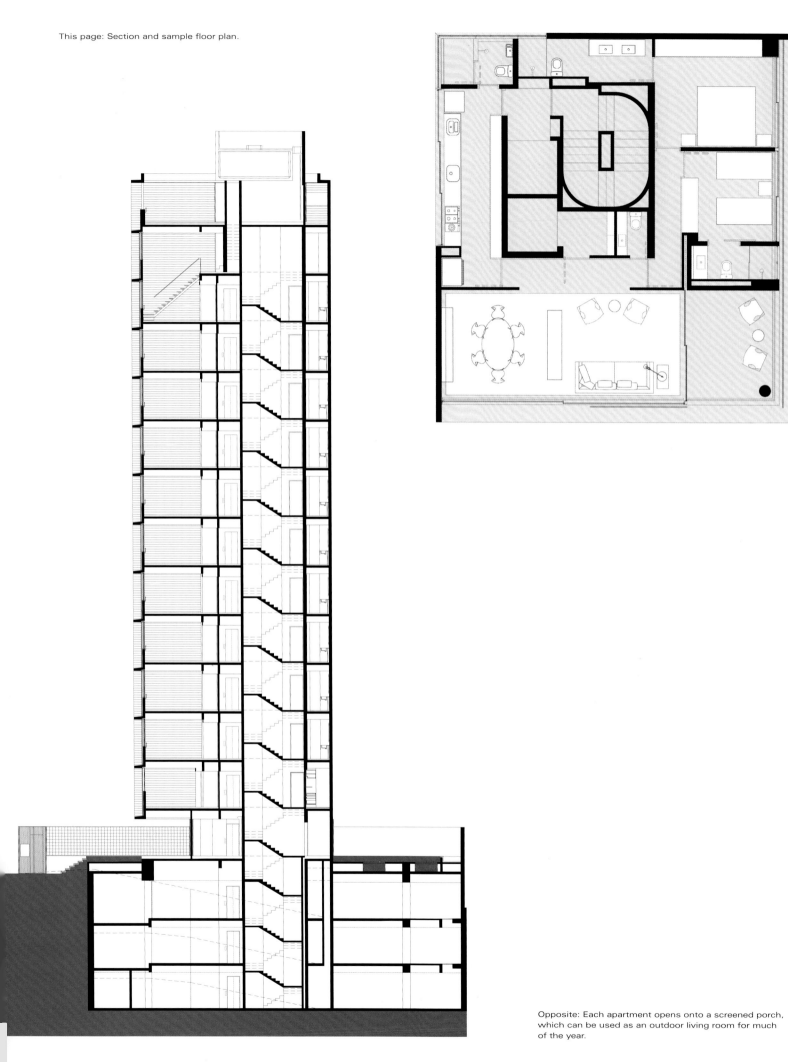

Opposite: Each apartment opens onto a screened porch, which can be used as an outdoor living room for much of the year.

Tiny square openings serve as vertical planters and echo the stones in the Venetian wall that surrounds the old city of Nicosia.

WHITE WALLS: GARDENS ALOFT

Stasinou 6, Nicosia, Cyprus

Ateliers Jean Nouvel
2004–14

The island of Cyprus has been divided into Greek and Turkish zones ever since the failed Greek coup and Turkish invasion of 1974. Although the border that divides the two extends through Nicosia, the capital ranks as one of the most prosperous in the world, and is a center of international banking. The residential tower of White Walls symbolizes this affluence. Dakis Joannou, the owner of Nice Day Developments, wanted to make an important contribution to the city he loves, and he began discussions with Ateliers Jean Nouvel in 2000. His goal was to create a complex of luxurious apartments, where he and members of his family would live, and a library he would donate to the university.

White Walls is aptly named: a slender, eighteen-story shaft of gleaming white concrete with pierced and open façades that respond to the hot summers (in which the temperature can top 104°F/40°C) and the temperate winters. At 220 ft (67 m), it is the tallest building in Nicosia, located on a small plot near Eleftheria Square and the zig-zag bastions that Venetian rulers erected around 1500 to protect the old city from attack by the Turks. Its height made it a sensitive issue, and although the surrounding buildings are mundane, Nouvel's design was rigorously scrutinized. "You can't do this" was the initial reaction, according to project architect Elizabeth Kather.

It took three years to secure planning permission and ten years from design to completion, even though it was the only building in the area to respect its surroundings. The scatter of tiny square openings in the east and west façades echo the stones in the Venetian wall. While some are glazed, others are left open, and the plantings that sprout from these apertures provide a visual link to a line of ancient olive trees and the public parks on three sides. Ironically, after construction began, the former height restriction was relaxed and the city permitted an additional two floors. There are three basement levels for parking and storage, a two-story retail base, six stories of offices, and ten levels of apartments. The construction budget grew from 5 to 11.5 million euros.

"It was a small job for AJN and we didn't have the budget to do research, but we worked with Arup and, even more productively, with a local engineer and Takis Sophocleous Architects," says Kather. The concept of different, climate-responsive façades softened by intensive plantings was explored in AJN's Hotel Renaissance Fira in Barcelona. The climate in Nicosia is hotter, however, so shade and cooling were critical issues. The pixelated openings in the poured white concrete walls were a challenge for the builders,

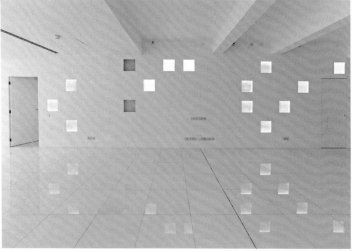

a problem they ingeniously solved with special scaffolding. The openings serve as scaling devices, reducing the mass of the building while disguising the different floor levels and the shift from offices to apartments. They also provide a brise-soleil and cooling device, as well as a protective screen for native plants, which emerge from the openings and are irrigated on a drip system that requires little attention from residents. The south side is treated as a living façade, where deciduous plantings provide shade in summer and shed their leaves to pull in the warmth of the sun in winter.

The ground plan is flared to add space, since the client determined that each one-floor apartment should be 3,230 sq ft (300 sq m)—the size of a middle-class family house. Bedrooms are ranged along the east and west sides and lit from the spaces behind the tiny openings. The central living areas open up to city through balconies to the north and south. These are staggered, in and out, to assure privacy. Residents hired their own interior designers; AJN, however, designed the client's duplex penthouse. This opens onto a central courtyard in the traditional Cypriot way, and three large canopies shade the roof terrace and pool from direct sun.

Although White Walls caters unabashedly to affluent residents, as does AJN's condo tower in lower Manhattan, the firm brings the same level of invention to social housing. Nemausus in Nîmes (page 23) has become a landmark—albeit a controversial one—and AJN has recently completed affordable apartment buildings in Nice, Bordeaux, and Mulhouse, as well as a student residence in Marseille.

The openings unify the block and mask the divide between the lower-level offices and upper-level apartments. Three canopies shade the rooftop pool.

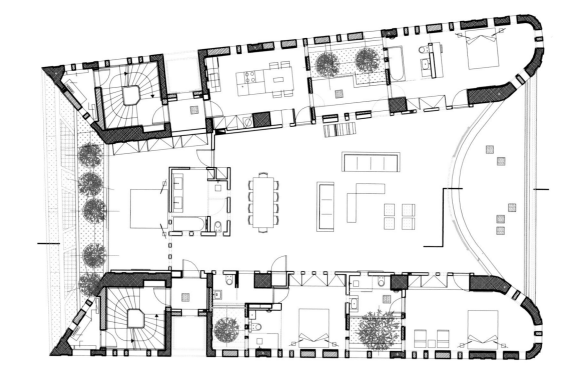

Opposite: The floor plan is flared to make best use of the
site, and each façade responds to the movement of the sun.
Right: North–south section.

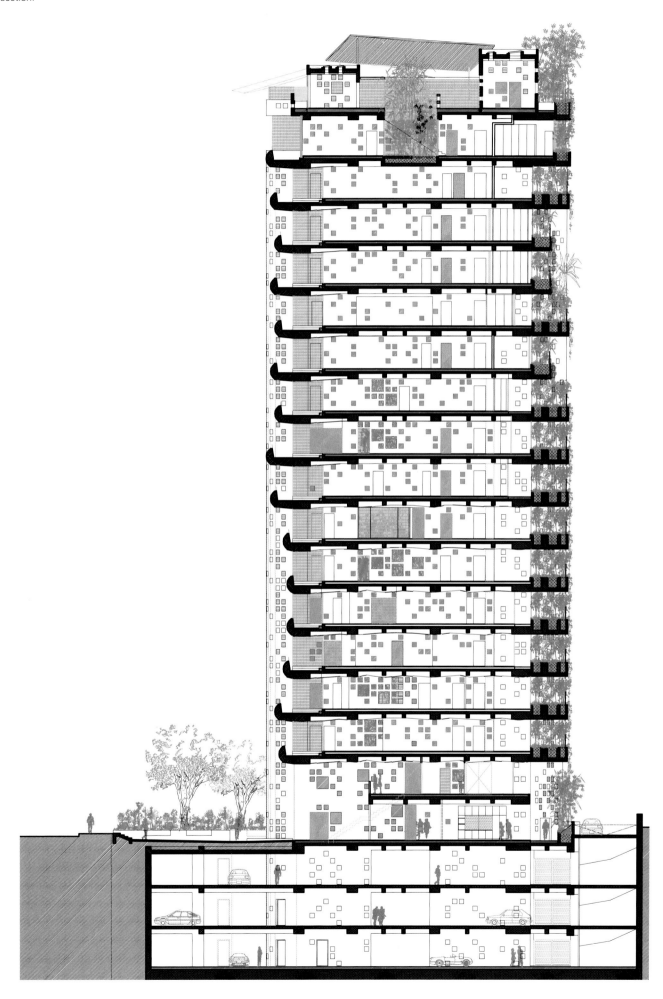

SKY HABITAT: STEPPING BACK

Bishan Street 15, Bishan, Singapore

**Safdie Architects
2011–15**

Sky Habitat is a recent example of Moshe Safdie's career-long quest to develop the ideas that he first explored in Montreal with Habitat 67 (pages 18–19). Early attempts to replicate that system of stacked prefabricated units failed to materialize and the architect moved in different directions, creating cultural and commercial buildings in Canada and around the world. Five decades on, he is trying a fresh approach. As he wrote back in 1970, "Since Habitat was completed, there has been a tendency to confuse two quite different ideas: the notion of the prefabricated space cell—a technological idea—and the notion of the reformed high-rise building, with its amenities and gardens, openness, and streets in the air—an environmental idea."

Safdie's Golden Dream Bay, a vast beachfront complex in the Chinese city of Qinhuangdao, is the ultimate expression of the concept of openness, with a continuous street system on different levels, but it is likely to become a sparsely peopled community of second homes. Sky Habitat, by contrast, is located on a densely populated island, and its 509 apartments are fully occupied. It had to conform to Singapore's strict height and environmental regulations. Two thirty-eight-story towers are linked at three levels by sky bridges that each provide a different experience for the residents. The fourteenth-level concourse is tree-shaded and contemplative, the twenty-sixth level is more open and playful, while the rooftop level is the most interactive, with an infinity pool, sports equipment, and sweeping views. More recreational amenities—including lap and leisure pools, tennis courts, a gym, and a screening room—are located at ground level. That makes the complex particularly appealing to families with children, as well as to residents who want an intensely social life.

To keep costs down, Mitsubishi contractors employed standard concrete-frame construction, but the product is anything but conventional. Each block is stepped back on one side and balconies project out at different angles to pull in more light and allow more headroom for private plantings. As with Habitat 67, the blocks are likely to become progressively greener over the next decade, since everything grows rapidly

in the tropics. CapitaLand, a developer that has also worked with UN Studio (Raffles City in Hangzhou), Steven Holl (Sliced Porosity in Chengdu), and Ole Scheeren (the Interlace, page 103), was open to new ideas. "They loved the concept of Habitat 67 and were eager to do something in that spirit, but they are tough," recalls Safdie. "We had to make the numbers work and be very innovative with vertical circulation. We were helped by a zoning ordinance (since changed) that excluded decks and other spaces that are open to the sky from the floor-to-ground-area ratio."

Sky Habitat is located in Bishan, an emerging neighborhood away from the center of Singapore and with a lot of public housing, factors that keep sale prices in the middle range. In planning the apartments, which range from a 680 sq ft (63 sq m) one-bedroom to 3,950 sq ft (367 sq m) penthouses, Safdie strove for a level of equity in the living environment. "At Habitat 67, every unit, high or low, is a good place to live," he insists. "Here, I wanted everybody to have a view, a measure of privacy, and not be blocked by neighboring buildings or suffer diminished light. That drove the design. We edited out anything that would result in second-class units—I find that unacceptable. Exciting forms are not enough." Although the density is much greater than in Montreal, the apartments have multiple orientations, cross-ventilation, and landscaped terraces that can be used year-round.

Could affordable housing have these same qualities? "I would welcome the challenge—though it would have to be done on a fairly big scale—of pushing the envelope to provide such amenities to lower-income residents," says Safdie. "It could happen in Asia if I were to find a sufficiently ambitious developer, or if I could persuade the Singapore Housing Authority to consider new typologies. I'd like to return to the idea of prefabrication, though not the modular boxes of Habitat 67, which are difficult to transport. Instead, there might be an assembly of smaller components, including factory-made bathrooms and kitchens." In the meantime, the architect continues to explore new solutions, with a sixty-five-story tower in Colombo, Sri Lanka; Parkside in Toronto; and a large, mixed-use scheme in the center of Chongqing.

An aerial view of the pool terrace that links the top level of the two stepped blocks, leaving swimmers suspended in midair.

Each of the three bridges that join the blocks plays a different role and serves all the residents as a space for recreation or relaxation.

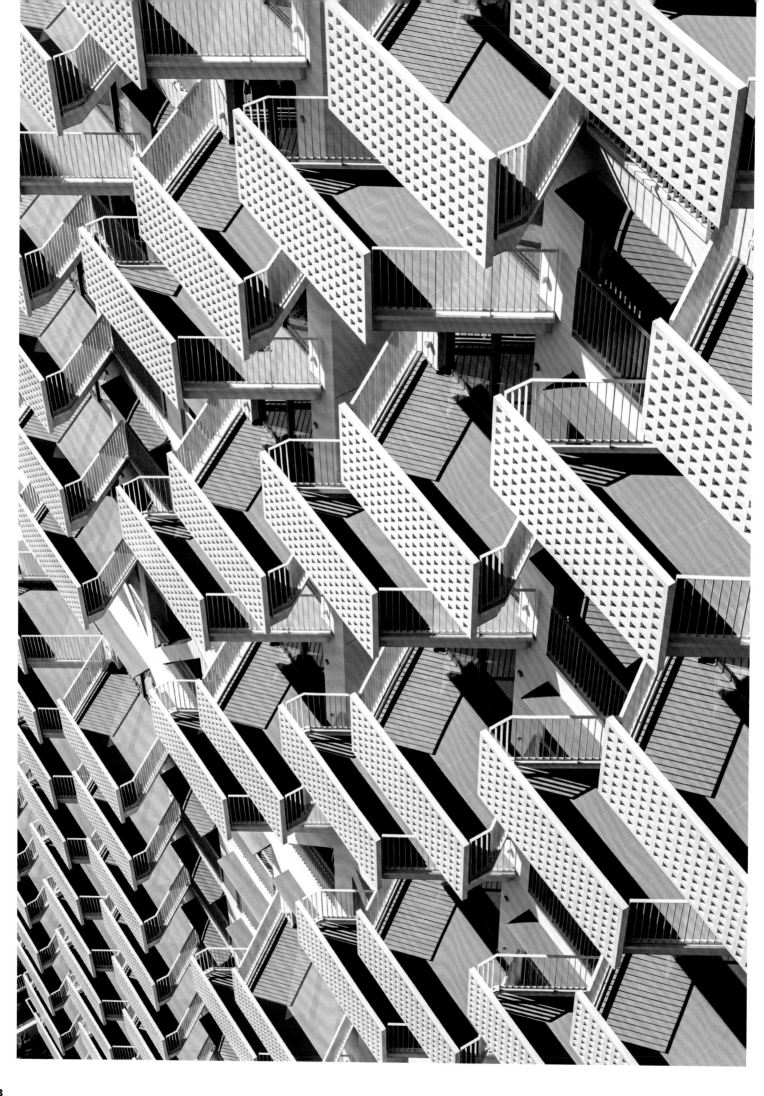

Opposite: Balconies are angled in different directions to enliven the profile and
give every resident greater privacy. Below: Sample floor plan and site plan.

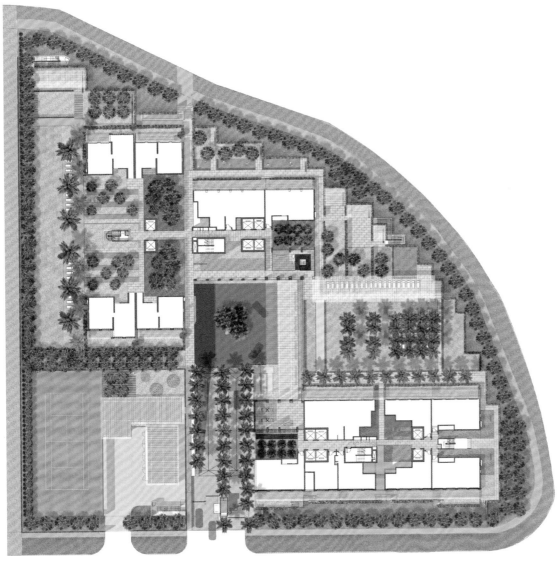

Maison Édouard François was established in Paris in 1998. Since then, it has designed a succession of green residential buildings in France and as far afield as India and China, alternating with the adaptive use of historic structures. Eitan Hammer, a partner of Édouard François, contributed to this interview.

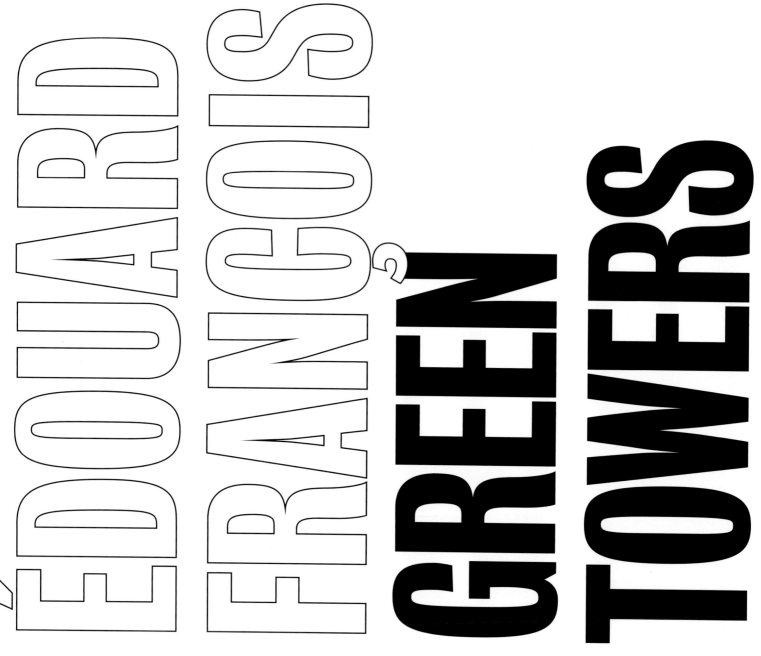

ÉDOUARD FRANÇOIS GREEN TOWERS

The Flower Tower, completed in 2004, employs planters of bamboo to immerse residents in greenery.

The Vertical Chameleon (2016) features plants that are native to rock crevices, embedding them in steel tubes that are an integral part of the façades.

"In 1999, I wrote in *Le Monde* that modernism had collapsed, and it would take a major economic crisis to spark a new approach, one that addressed issues of sustainability. When I taught at the AA [the Architectural Association in London], I explored the potential of green architecture, which would be in harmony with nature. I started building in the countryside—initially, it was more about context than a guy putting plants on a building.

"I've done about twenty apartment buildings and each is a demonstration of a particular idea. I don't want to repeat myself. The hardest thing is to convince a client to take a chance on innovation—although I never use that word with them. When you add plants, you can save as much as 30 percent on the cost of the façades. There's a strong emphasis on efficiency and the happiness of the residents. All my buildings have high LEED [environmental certification] ratings.

"Over the past ten years I've realized that Paris has to 'densify,' which means building higher on the edge of the city. The mayor, Anne Hidalgo, promised to build 10,000 social housing units—half of which have been realized. The problem is cost and the shortage of space. I moved to an eleventh-floor duplex apartment myself. Then I realized that the rich guys live at the top and the poorer residents below. If we build high we have to share altitude—giving the lower stories larger balconies—and allowing everyone access to the roof. I'm doing that in a building now under construction in Grenoble, where north-facing apartments have south-facing balconies. I'm creating an urban farm with a glass roof at the center of Paris, and a tower on pilotis in Bordeaux, in which the sheltered area below is a farm with chickens.

"I'm dealing with materiality and human values. The Flower Tower [completed in 2004 on the outer edge of the 17th arrondissement] erased the boundary between the building and a park. The pots of bamboo around the periphery, which soften the impact of the tower, were inspired by Parisian window planters. In the newly completed Tour de la Biodiversité [an eighteen-story tower of ninety-five units dubbed the Vertical Chameleon], we've incorporated fast-growing creepers as well as trees that will take years to grow out, and in twenty years we will plant oaks that will need even longer to mature. I said I was creating a green mountain, using seeds from forests in the Île de France. They require little water and withstand high winds—which makes them ideal for tall buildings.

"The Vertical Chameleon is built beside a highway over a railway tunnel in the 13th arrondissement, to the rear of the Très Grande Bibliothèque. We collaborated with the Jardin des Plantes [JdP] to discover what grows best at a height of 160 ft [50 m]. We were told to look at plants with long roots that grow in mountain crevices. We tried to recreate that habitat with 11 ft [3.5 m] long steel tubes filled with earth, which contain the roots, like planters. Irrigation is incorporated into the handrail. Everything was tested for three years at the JdP—for temperature variations from 32 to 104°F [0 to 40°C].

"At every level we double the number of tubes, with a continuous planter at roof level. It's like a tree—from bare trunk to an exuberant top. We've achieved a much higher degree of integration between nature and structure than before—the culmination of a decade of work. Planters are located on a second, 2 ft [60 cm] wide balcony, like a peripheral catwalk, to ensure they are cared for, since this is social housing. It's much more delicate than bamboo—and JdP will be making an inspection every four months. A crystallized titanium façade serves as a backdrop to the vegetation tubes, while a net climbing-frame doubles as a balustrade and serves as a veil that adds a layer to the building. We made economies in order to afford this material."

The following pages showcase
a sampling of projects that—at
the time of writing—are under
construction, awaiting approval,
or concepts for future development.
They illustrate varied strategies for
breaking out of the box, opening
up living spaces for residents,
and enriching the environment.

LOOKING AHEAD

THE VILLAGE, ALIBAUG

Sanjay Puri Architects

The Village is a complex of apartments that cascade down a steep slope in the coastal town of Alibaug, 60 miles (100 km) south of Mumbai, India. Inspired by the organic structure of old Indian cities, Sanjay Puri Architects has preserved the natural contours of the land to give each unit a sheltered terrace and open garden. The linked blocks are oriented to the north, and will be constructed from locally quarried basalt, which provides good insulation and gives the complex a strong feeling of place.

8600 WILSHIRE, BEVERLY HILLS

MAD Architects

8600 Wilshire is MAD's first US project: an eighteen-unit residential cluster atop commercial space, located on a busy boulevard in Beverly Hills. Inspired by the houses that climb the Hollywood Hills, it comprises a mix of studios, condos, and translucent-glass villas that open onto a lushly planted courtyard. From the street, a green wall of drought-tolerant succulents and vines seems to float above the glass storefronts. The complex is scaled to the low-rise neighborhood and should be completed in 2017.

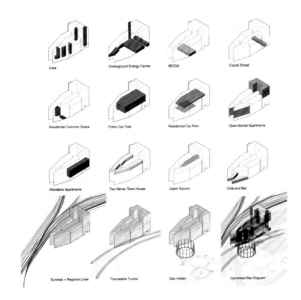

THE TAPESTRY, LONDON

Niall McLaughlin Architects

The Tapestry was designed by Niall McLaughlin Architects
as a multi-use block sandwiched between the Channel
Tunnel Rail Link and a main rail line in the new 32 acre (13 ha)
development behind St. Pancras and King's Cross stations
in London. Shaped by program and site, the bold modeling
is enriched with pigmented precast concrete panels and
columns that employ CADCAM technology to reproduce
a variety of historical ornament. Residents will enjoy sweeping
views, in-house amenities, and a rooftop garden.

ECKWERK, BERLIN

GRAFT

Eckwerk was designed by GRAFT and Kleihues+Kleihues as a dynamic, mixed-use complex on a triangular site flanking the Stadtbahn, the elevated railway that runs through Berlin. Five towers are linked by a raised pedestrian route and a glass-roofed atrium. The multistory marketplace in the podium takes its cues from the arches of the viaduct and creates a lively bustle beneath the affordable rental units in the towers. These are conceived as live–work spaces, and the project is due for completion in 2018.

MAES-EN-BOERENBOOMPLEIN, KNOKKE-HEIST

Jakob + MacFarlane

Maes-en-Boerenboomplein takes its name from a marketplace in the Belgian seaside resort of Knokke-Heist. Jakob + MacFarlane has designed a mixed-use block of apartments and commercial and civic facilities that will provide a community meeting house that residents and locals can share. To break up the mass, a collage of distinct elements is contained within the reinforced-concrete frame. The building also serves as a model of sustainable design and construction, with low energy consumption, and as a colorful complement to the old town hall.

TREE HOUSE

Rogers Stirk Harbour + Partners

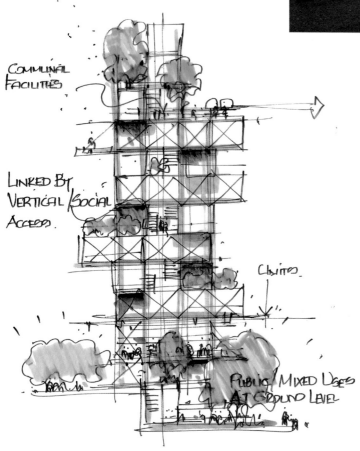

Communal Facilities

Linked By Vertical Social Access.

Clusters.

Public Mixed Uses at Ground Level

Tree House is a conceptual design for the rapid assembly of low-cost apartments, developed by Rogers Stirk Harbour + Partners for the 2016 Venice Biennale, that draws on the firm's experience in creating modular housing in London. Conceived as a simple kit of parts that can be locally sourced, it stacks 800 sq ft (75 sq m) timber-framed living units around a central staircase and elevator up to ten stories high. The configuration can be adapted to a diversity of sites, and each unit has a flexible internal layout.

BEIRUT TERRACES, BEIRUT

Herzog & de Meuron

Beirut Terraces expresses the resilience and hedonism
of the much-scarred Lebanese capital, which was once
a cosmopolitan resort. Herzog & de Meuron has created
a 390 ft (119 m) high tower of upscale condos in which
slender floor plates shift from one side to another and seem
to be cantilevered into space as outdoor stages for the
glass-walled living areas. There is a mix of apartment types,
all of which exploit the benign climate of Beirut and contribute
to the revitalization of this particular quarter of the city.

L'ARBRE BLANC, MONTPELLIER

Sou Fujimoto Architects

L'Arbre Blanc is a seventeen-story mixed-use tower in Montpellier, a provincial capital in the South of France that has enjoyed spectacular growth in recent decades. Sou Fujimoto collaborated with two young French architects—Manal Rachdi and Nicolas Laisné—in designing this white tree of 105 varied apartments, each with a dramatically extended terrace. They rise from a base of offices, restaurant, bar, and art gallery, making this a vibrant new addition to the city's array of contemporary architectural showpieces.

PROJECT R6, SEOUL

REX

Project R6 is a complex of studio apartments over a retail base, located in a new business district of Seoul. To maximize exposure to light, cross-ventilation, and views, REX has stretched the conventional tower laterally to create a cage of vertical and horizontal elements surrounding a void. Each unit is fully furnished and equipped for short stays by businesspeople and foreigners. The project is currently on hold, but it has the potential to redefine urban living and the city skyline.

FURTHER READING

John Allan, *Berthold Lubetkin: Architecture and the Tradition of Progress* (London: Black Dog), 2012

Andrew Benner, Nina Rappaport, and James Andrachuk (eds.), *Social Infrastructure: New York—Douglas Durst and Bjarke Ingels* (New York: Actar), 2015

Nicholas Dagen Bloom and Mathew Gordon Lasner (eds.), *Affordable Housing in New York: The People, Places, and Policies that Transformed a City* (Princeton, NJ: Princeton University Press), 2015

Karla Britton, *Auguste Perret* (London and New York: Phaidon), 2001

Carles Broto, *Apartment Buildings Today* (Barcelona: Links), 2011

Jean-Louis Cohen, *The Future of Architecture, Since 1889* (London and New York: Phaidon), 2012

Kenneth Frampton, *Modern Architecture: A Critical History*, 4th edn. (London and New York: Thames & Hudson), 2007

Paul Groenendijk, *Architectuurgids Nederland: 1900–2000 = Architectural Guide to the Netherlands, 1900–2000* (Rotterdam: 010 Publishers), 2006

La cité du Lignon, 1963–1971: Étude architecturale et stratégies d'intervention (Geneva: Infolio), 2012

Le Corbusier: Architect of the Century (London: Arts Council of Great Britain), 1987

François Loyer and Hélène Guéné, *Henri Sauvage: Les immeubles à gradins = Henri Sauvage: Set-Back Buildings* (Liège: Mardaga), 1987

Landesdenkmalamt Berlin (ed.), *Siedlungen der Berliner Moderne: Eintragung in die Welterbeliste der UNESCO = Berlin Modernism Housing Estates: Inscription on the UNESCO World Heritage List* (Berlin: Braun), 2009

Rowan Moore, *Slow Burn City: London in the Twenty-First Century* (London: Pan Macmillan), 2016

Museum Het Schip, *Workers' Palace: The Ship by Michel de Klerk* (Amsterdam: Museum Het Schip), 2012

Styliane Philippou, *Oscar Niemeyer: Curves of Irreverence* (New Haven, Conn.: Yale University Press), 2008

Alan Powers, *Modern: The Modern Movement in Britain* (London and New York: Merrell), 2005

Moshe Safdie, *Beyond Habitat by 20 Years* (Montreal: Tundra Books), 1987

Karel Teige, *The Minimum Dwelling* [1932], trans. Eric Dluhosch (Cambridge, Mass: MIT Press), 2002

Chris van Uffelen, *Apartment Buildings* (Salenstein: Braun), 2013

PICTURE CREDITS

Introduction: Evolution of a Typology

Urban Villages

Carabanchel Housing, Madrid: Roland Halbe and
Nic Lehoux, courtesy Morphosis; aerial courtesy
Ayunimento de Madrid
Nishinoyama House, Kyoto: Iwan Baan
Baroque Court Apartments, Ljubljana: Tomaž Gregori,
courtesy OFIS Arhitekti
25 Verde, Turin: Beppe Giardino, courtesy Luciano Pia
Boréal, Nantes: S. Chalmeau, courtesy Tetrarc
Broadway Housing, Santa Monica, California: Principal
photography by Iwan Baan; interior by Nico Marques/Photekt

Lorcan O'Herlihy: Reaching Out
Lawrence Anderson, courtesy LOH Architects

Building Blocks

CityLife, Milan: Iwan Baan and Michele Nastasi
De Kameleon, Amsterdam: Principal photography by Luuk
Kramer; interior and courtyard by Marcel van der Burg;
courtesy NL Architects
City Hyde Park, Chicago: Steve Hall/Hedrick Blessing,
courtesy Studio Gang
Studio 11024, Los Angeles: Iwan Baan
8 House, Copenhagen: Principal photography by Iwan Baan;
staircase image courtesy Bjarke Ingels Group/BIG
The Interlace, Singapore: Principal photography by Iwan
Baan; interior courtesy CapitaLand

Bjarke Ingels: Exploiting Irregularity
Courtesy Bjarke Ingels Group/BIG

Promoting Sociability

Tietgen, Copenhagen: Jens Lindhe, courtesy Lungaard
& Tranberg Arkitekter
The Commons, Brunswick: Principal photography by
Andrew Wuttke; lobby fire pipes and façade detail Michael
Downes/UA Creative; courtesy Breathe Architecture
Star Apartments, Los Angeles: Iwan Baan
Torr Kaelan, San Diego, California: Principal photography
by Darren Bradley, courtesy Rob Wellington Quigley, FAIA
Hérold, Paris: Cap Paysage and Nicholas Borel, courtesy
Jakob + MacFarlane Architects; wide view James Ewing/
OTTO
Songpa Micro Housing, Seoul: courtesy Single
Speed Design/SsD

Michael Maltzan: Housing for All
Carver exterior: Iwan Baan; courtyard image and Crest:
courtesy Michael Maltzan Architecture

Spirit of Place

Sugar Hill, New York: Principal photography by Ed Reeves,
courtesy Adjaye Associates; portrait of jazz saxophonist
James Rooke at home: Emile Dubuisson
The Wave, Vejle: Exterior photography by Thomas Moelvig,
interiors by Jesper Ray; courtesy Henning Larsen Architects
8 Octavia, San Francisco: Principal photography by Bruce
Damonte; aerial by Steve Proehl; courtesy Stanley Saitowitz/
Natoma Architects
The Aleph, Buenos Aires: Nigel Young, courtesy
Foster + Partners
HL 23, New York: Benny Chan, courtesy
Neil M. Denari Architects
JOH 3, Berlin: Ludger Paffrath, courtesy J. Mayer H.

Stanley Saitowitz: Rigorous Strategies
Bruce Damonte, courtesy Stanley Saitowitz/
Natoma Architects

Reaching Skyward

8 Spruce Street, New York: courtesy Forest City
Ratner Companies/dbox
Absolute Towers, Mississauga: Iwan Baan, courtesy
MAD Architects
Marco Polo Tower, Hamburg: Roland Halbe, courtesy
Behnisch Architekten
V_Itaim, São Paolo: Photography by Pedro Vannucchi,
courtesy Studio MK27
White Walls, Nicosia: Yiorgis Gerolymbos, courtesy
Nice Day Developments
Sky Habitat, Singapore: Edward Hendricks, courtesy
Safdie Architects

Maison Édouard François: Green Towers
Courtesy Maison Édouard François

Looking Ahead

The Village, Alibaug: Sanjay Puri Architects
8600 Wilshire, Beverly Hills: MAD Architects
The Tapestry, London: Wide view, Miller Hare; diagram,
Niall McLaughlin Architects; detail, PicturePlane
Eckwerk, Berlin: GRAFT
Maes-en-Boerenboomplein, Knokke-Heist:
Jakob + MacFarlane
Tree House: Rogers Stirk Harbor + Partners
Beirut Terraces, Beirut: Herzog & de Meuron
L'Arbre Blanc, Montpellier: Sou Fujimoto Architects
Project R6, Seoul: REX

INDEX

Bold page numbers indicate main illustrated entries for case study buildings; *italic* page numbers refer to other illustrations.